# SUPPLEMENT

## TO

## *A Manual of French Composition*

# SUPPLEMENT

## TO

# *A Manual of French Composition*

BY

## R. L. GRÆME RITCHIE, D.Litt.

*Professor of French in the University of Birmingham*

AND

## JAMES M. MOORE, M.A.

*Lecturer in French in the University of Edinburgh*

CAMBRIDGE
AT THE UNIVERSITY PRESS
1922

# CAMBRIDGE
## UNIVERSITY PRESS

University Printing House, Cambridge CB2 8BS, United Kingdom

Cambridge University Press is part of the University of Cambridge.

It furthers the University's mission by disseminating knowledge in the pursuit of education, learning and research at the highest international levels of excellence.

www.cambridge.org
Information on this title: www.cambridge.org/9781316619940

First published 1922
First paperback edition 2016

A catalogue record for this publication is available from the British Library

ISBN 978-1-316-61994-0 Paperback

# PREFACE

THIS *Supplement* to our *Manual of French Composition*
(1914) is intended to meet the wants of teachers who, like
ourselves, have now nearly worked through the Passages for
Translation. The two hundred additional pieces here printed
have been selected on the same principle as those in the
*Manual*, and are arranged in the same way. Many of them
we have already used ourselves, in class or for examination
purposes; the remainder are the most instructive of those which
from time to time we have noted as containing important
points in translation and illustrating the differences between
French and English prose style.

R. L. G. R.
J. M. M.

*September* 1922.

# TABLE OF CONTENTS

Acknowledgements are due to the following Authors and Publishers, who have kindly allowed us to print extracts from the undernoted copyright works :—

Mr Max Beerbohm and Messrs Wm. Heinemann, *And Even Now*.

Mr Hilaire Belloc and Messrs George Allen & Unwin, Ltd., *The Path to Rome*.

Messrs Wm. Blackwood & Sons, Dr John Kerr's *Memories Grave and Gay*.

Mr J. E. C. Bodley and Messrs Longmans, Green & Co., *The Decay of Idealism in France*.

Mr J. E. C. Bodley and Messrs Macmillan & Co. Ltd., *France*.

Mr John Buchan and Messrs John Lane The Bodley Head Limited, *A Lost Lady of Old Years*.

Mr Edward Carpenter and Messrs George Allen & Unwin, Ltd., *England's Ideal*.

Messrs Cassell & Co. Ltd., R. L. Stevenson's *Kidnapped*.

Messrs Chatto & Windus, R. L. Stevenson's *An Inland Voyage, The Merry Men, Travels with a Donkey*.

Mr Joseph Conrad and Messrs Methuen & Co. Ltd., *The Mirror of the Sea*.

Messrs Constable & Company Limited, Joseph Chamberlain's *Speeches* ; Messrs Constable & Company Limited and Charles Scribner's Sons, New York, George Meredith's *The Adventures of Harry Richmond, The Egoist, Vittoria*.

Mr Robert Dell and Messrs John Lane The Bodley Head Limited, *My Second Country*.

Sir Arthur Conan Doyle and Mr John Murray, *The White Company*.

Sir James G. Frazer and Messrs Macmillan & Co. Ltd., *The Golden Bough* and *Pausanias*.

Mr R. B. Cunninghame Graham and Messrs Duckworth & Co., *Scottish Stories*.

Mr Stephen Gwynn and Messrs Maunsell & Co. Ltd., *For Second Reading*.

Mrs E. Hamerton and Messrs Seeley, Service & Co. Ltd., Philip Gilbert Hamerton's *Round My House*.

Mr Thomas Hardy and Messrs Macmillan & Co. Ltd., *The Return of the Native*.

Messrs Harper & Brothers, Henry James's *Essays in London and Elsewhere*.

Mr James Joyce and The Egoist Press, *A Portrait of the Artist as a Young Man*.

Mr Rudyard Kipling and Messrs Macmillan & Co., Ltd., *France at War*.

Mr E. A. Greening Lamborn and Messrs Methuen & Co. Ltd., *The Teaching of English Literature*, in *The Modern Teacher*.

Messrs Longmans, Green & Co., J. A. Froude's *Oceana*.

Messrs Macmillan & Co. Ltd., J. R. Green's *History of the English People*; P. G. Hamerton's *The Intellectual Life*.

Messrs Methuen & Co. Ltd., Oscar Wilde's *The Canterville Ghost*.

Viscount Morley of Blackburn and Messrs Macmillan & Co. Ltd., *Burke*.

Mr John Murray, Mrs Humphry Ward's *The Marriage of William Ashe*.

Sir Henry Newbolt, Miss Mary Coleridge's *The King is dead*.

Mr Frank Norris and Messrs Thomas Nelson & Sons, Limited, *The Pit*.

The Oratorian Fathers, Birmingham, Cardinal J. H. Newman's *A Grammar of Assent*.

The representatives of the late George Gissing through Mr James B. Pinker, *The Private Papers of Henry Ryecroft*.

The-Right Hon. The Earl of Rosebery, *Napoleon: The Last Phase*.

Messrs Seeley, Service & Co. Ltd., R. L. Stevenson's *Edinburgh*.

Mr James Stephens and Messrs Macmillan & Co. Ltd., *The Charwoman's Daughter*, *The Crock of Gold*, *The Demi-Gods*, *Irish Fairy Tales*.

Sir Rabindranath Tagore and Messrs Macmillan & Co. Ltd., *My Reminiscences*.

Mrs Rachel Annand Taylor and the Editor of *Alma Mater*, *The Coming of the Women Students*.

Mr H. G. Wells, *Kipps*, *The History of Mr Polly*, *Mr Britling sees it through*.

Mr W. B. Yeats and Messrs Macmillan & Co. Ltd., *Ideas of Good and Evil*.

# PASSAGES FOR TRANSLATION

\* Easy.  \*\* Moderately difficult.  \*\*\* Difficult.
\*\*\*\* Very difficult.

## I. DESCRIPTIVE

### 1.\*\* SUNRISE.

I must not close my letter without giving you one principal event of my history, which was that—in the course of my late tour—I set out one morning before five o'clock, the moon shining through a dark and misty autumnal air, and got to the sea-coast time enough to be at the sun's levee. I saw the clouds and dark vapours open gradually to right and left, rolling over one another in great smoky wreaths, and the tide —as it flowed gently in upon the sands—first whitening, then slightly tinged with gold and blue; and all at once a little line of insufferable brightness that—before I can write these five words—was grown to half an orb, and now to a whole one, too glorious to be distinctly seen. It is very odd it makes no figure on paper; yet I shall remember it as long as the sun, or at least as long as I can endure. I wonder whether anybody ever saw it before. I hardly believe it.

THOMAS GRAY, *Letters*.

### 2.\*\* MORNING.

He got up presently, and stood quite motionless at the window, looking out.

His lamp was still burning, but for some time he had not been writing by the light of his lamp. Insensibly the day had come and abolished his need for that individual circle of yellow light. Colour had returned to the world, clean pearly colour, clear and definite like the glance of a child or the voice of a girl, and a golden wisp of cloud hung in the sky over the tower of the church. There was a mist upon the pond, a soft grey mist not a yard high. A covey of partridges ran and halted and ran again in the dewy grass outside his garden railings. The partridges were very numerous this year because there had been so little shooting. Beyond, in the meadow, a hare sat up as still as a stone. A horse neighed.

Wave after wave of warmth and light came sweeping before the sunrise across the world of Matching's Easy. It was as if there was nothing but morning and sunrise in the world.

From away towards the church came the sound of some early worker whetting a scythe.

H. G. WELLS, *Mr Britling sees it through.*

### 3.** THE CHANGING DAY.

Every morning as I awoke, I somehow felt the day coming to me like a new gilt-edged letter, with some unheard-of news awaiting me on the opening of the envelope. And, lest I should lose any fragment of it, I would hurry through my toilet to my chair outside. Every day there was the ebb and flow of the tide on the Ganges; the various gait of so many different boats; the shifting of the shadows of the trees from west to east; and, over the fringe of shade-patches of the woods on the opposite bank, the gush of golden life-blood through the pierced breast of the evening sky. Some days would be cloudy from early morning; the opposite woods black; black shadows moving over the river. Then with a rush would come the vociferous rain, blotting out the horizon; the dim line of the other bank taking its leave in tears: the river swelling with suppressed heavings; and the moist wind making free with the foliage of the trees overhead.

Sir RABINDRANATH TAGORE, *My Reminiscences.*

### 4.*** A NOVEMBER AFTERNOON.

A Saturday afternoon in November was approaching the time of twilight, and the vast tract of unenclosed wild known as Egdon Heath embrowned itself moment by moment. Overhead the hollow stretch of whitish cloud shutting out the sky was as a tent which had the whole heath for its floor.

The heaven being spread with this pallid screen and the earth with the darkest vegetation, their meeting-line at the horizon was clearly marked. In such contrast the heath wore the appearance of an instalment of night which had taken up its place before its astronomical hour was come: darkness had to a great extent arrived hereon, while day stood distinct in the sky. Looking upwards, a furze-cutter would have been inclined to continue work; looking down, he would have decided to finish his faggot and go home. The distant rims of the world and of the firmament seemed to be a division in time no less than a division in matter. The face of the heath by its mere complexion added half an hour to evening; it could in like manner retard the dawn, sadden noon, anticipate the frowning of storms scarcely generated, and intensify the opacity of a moonless midnight to a cause of shaking and dread.

THOMAS HARDY, *The Return of the Native.*

### 5.** TWILIGHT.

The day had drawn to its close. The stars had not yet come, nor the moon. Far to the west a red cloud poised on the horizon like a great whale and, moment by moment, it paled and faded until it was no more than a pink flush. On high, clouds of pearl and snow piled and fell and sailed away on easy voyages. It was the twilight—a twilight of such quietude that one could hear the soft voice of the world as it whispered through leaf and twig. There was no breeze to swing the branches of the trees or to creep among the rank grasses and set them dancing, and yet everywhere there was unceasing movement and a sound that never ceased. About them, for mile upon mile, there was no habitation of man; there was no movement anywhere except when a bird dipped and soared in a hasty flight homewards, or when a beetle went slugging by like a tired bullet.

JAMES STEPHENS, *The Demi-Gods.*

### 6.** A Midsummer Night.

With every step upward a greater mystery surrounded me. A few stars were out, and the brown night mist was creeping along the water below: but there was still light enough to see the road, and even to distinguish the bracken in the deserted hollows. The highway became little better than a lane: at the top of a hill it plunged under the tall pines, and was vaulted over with darkness. The kingdoms that have no walls, and are built up of shadows, began to oppress me as the night hardened. Had I had companions, still we would only have spoken in a whisper, and in that dungeon of trees, even my own self would not raise its voice within me.

It was full night when I had reached a vague clearing in the woods, right up on the height of that flat hill. This clearing was called "The Fountain of Magdalen." I was so far relieved by the broader sky of the open field that I could wait and rest a little and there, at last, separate from men, I thought of a thousand things.

HILAIRE BELLOC, *The Path to Rome.*

### 7.** A Midsummer Night (*continued*).

The air was full of midsummer, and its mixture of exaltation and fear cut me off from ordinary living. I now understood why our religion has made sacred this season of the year; why we have, a little later, the night of St John, the fires in the villages, and the old perception of fairies dancing in the rings of the summer grass. A general communion of all things conspires at this crisis of summer against us reasoning men that should live in the daylight, and something fantastic possesses those who are foolish enough to watch upon such nights.

So I, watching, was cut off. There were huge, vague summits, all wooded, peering above the field I sat in, but they merged into a confused horizon. I was on a high plateau, yet I felt myself to be alone with the immensity that properly belongs to plains alone. I saw the stars, and remembered how

I had looked up at them on just such a night when I was close to the Pacific, bereft of friends and possessed with solitude. There was no noise; it was full darkness. The woods before and behind me made a square frame of silence, and I was enchased here in the clearing, thinking of all things.

HILAIRE BELLOC, The Path to Rome.

### 8.* A COLD NIGHT-JOURNEY.

The night and the snow came on together, and dismal enough they were. There was no sound to be heard but the howling of the wind, for the noise of the wheels and the tread of the horses' feet were rendered inaudible by the thick coating of snow which covered the earth, and was fast increasing every moment. The streets of Stamford were deserted as they passed through the town ; and its old churches rose, frowning and dark, from the whitened ground. Twenty miles farther on, two of the front outside passengers, wisely availing themselves of their arrival at one of the best inns in England, turned in for the night at the 'George' at Grantham. The remainder wrapped themselves more closely in their coats and cloaks, and leaving the light and warmth of the town behind them, pillowed themselves against the luggage, and prepared, with many half-suppressed moans, again to encounter the piercing blast which swept across the open country.

CHARLES DICKENS, Nicholas Nickleby.

### 9.* THE SHAP GRADIENT.

They passed by Lancaster, skirting the sea on which the moon shone bright, setting the fishing-boats in silver as they lay scarcely moving on the waves. Then, so to speak, the train set its face up against Shap Fell, and, puffing heavily, drew up into the hills, the scattered grey stone houses of the north, flanked by their gnarled and twisted ash trees, hanging upon the edge of the streams, as lonely, and as cut off from the world (except the passing train) as they had been in Central Africa. The moorland roads, winding amongst the heather, showed that the feet of generations had marked them out, and not the line, spade and theodolite, with all the circumstance of modern road makers. They, too, looked white and unearthly in the moonlight, and now and then a sheep, aroused by the snorting of the train, moved from the heather into the middle of the road, and stood there motionless, its shadow filling the narrow track, and flickering on the heather at the edge.

R. B. Cunninghame Graham,
*Scottish Stories (Beattock for Moffat).*

### 10.*** The East Coast of Scotland.

Nothing is wilder than the long stretch of sandy coast which runs from the East Neuk of Fife right up to Aberdeen.

Inland, the wind-swept fields, with their rough walls, without a kindly feal upon the top, as in the west, look grim and un-inviting in their well-farmed ugliness.

The trees are low and stunted, and grow twisted by the prevailing fierce east winds, all to one side, just like the trees so often painted by the Japanese upon a fan.

The fields run down, until they lose themselves in sandy links, clothed with a growth of bent.

After the links, there intervenes a shingly beach, protected here and there by a low reef of rocks, all honeycombed and limpet-ridden, from which streamers of dulse float in the ceaseless surge.

Then comes the sea, grey, sullen, always on the watch to swallow up the fishermen, whose little brown-sailed boats seem to be scudding ceaselessly before the easterly haar towards some harbour's mouth.

Grey towns, with houses roofed with slabs of stone, cluster round little churches built so strongly that they have weathered reformations and the storms of centuries.

Grey sky, grey sullen sea, grey rocks, and a keen whistling wind that blows from the North Sea, which seems to turn the very air a steely grey, have given to the land a look of hardness not to be equalled upon earth.

R. B. Cunninghame Graham, *Scottish Stories (A Princess).*

## 11.* An Orkney Seascape.

From the top of Wideford Hill nearly all the islands may be seen; and no one who goes there on a clear day will hesitate to admit that the scene before him, looking seaward, is one of exquisite beauty. In calm weather the sea, land-locked by the islands, resembles a vast lake, clear and bright as a mirror, and without a ripple save from the gentle impulse of the tide. Here a bluff headland stands out in bold relief against the horizon, there the more distant islet is almost lost in sea and sky; on one side a shelving rock sends out a black tongue-like point, sharp as a needle, losing itself in the water where it forms one of those reefs so fatal to strangers, but which every Orkney boatman knows as we do the streets of our native town.

Dr JOHN KERR, *Memories Grave and Gay.*

## 12.** Wolf's Crag.

The roar of the sea had long announced their approach to the cliffs, on the summit of which, like the nest of some sea-eagle, the founder of the fortalice had perched his eyry. The pale moon, which had hitherto been contending with flitting clouds, now shone out, and gave them a view of the solitary and naked tower, situated on a projecting cliff that beetled on the German Ocean.

On three sides the rock was precipitous; on the fourth, which was that towards the land, it had been originally fenced by an artificial ditch and drawbridge, but the latter was broken down and ruinous, and the former had been in part filled up, so as to allow passage for a horseman into the narrow courtyard, encircled on two sides with low offices and stables, partly ruinous, and closed on the landward front by a low embattled wall, while the remaining side of the quadrangle was occupied by the tower itself, which, tall and narrow, and built of a greyish stone, stood glimmering in the moonlight, like the sheeted spectre of some huge giant.

A wilder or more disconsolate dwelling, it was perhaps

difficult to conceive. The sombrous and heavy sound of the billows, successively dashing against the rocky beach at a profound distance beneath, was to the ear what the landscape was to the eye—a symbol of unvaried and monotonous melancholy, not unmingled with horror.

Sir WALTER SCOTT, The Bride of Lammermoor.

## 13.* THE BREAKING OF THE STORM.

The crags which rose between the beach and the mainland, to the height of two or three hundred feet, afforded in their crevices shelter for unnumbered sea-fowl, in situations seemingly secured by their dizzy height from the rapacity of man. Many of these wild tribes, with the instinct which sends them to seek the land before a storm arises, were now winging towards their nests with the shrill and dissonant clang which announces disquietude and fear.

The disk of the sun became almost totally obscured ere he had altogether sunk below the horizon, and an early and lurid shade of darkness blotted the serene twilight of a summer evening. The wind began next to arise; but its wild and moaning sound was heard for some time, and its effects became visible on the bosom of the sea, before the gale was felt on shore. The mass of waters, now dark and threatening, began to lift itself in larger ridges, and sink in deeper furrows, forming waves that rose high in foam upon the breakers, or burst upon the beach with a sound resembling distant thunder.

Sir WALTER SCOTT, The Antiquary.

## 14.* A LONELY BOAT.

In returning from a cruise to the English coast, you see often enough a fisherman's humble boat far away from all shores, with an ugly black sky above, and an angry sea beneath; you watch the grisly old man at the helm carrying his craft with strange skill through the turmoil of waters, and the boy, supple-limbed, yet weather-worn already, and with

steady eyes that look through the blast; you see him under-
standing commandments from the jerk of his father's white
eyebrow....Stale enough is the sight, and yet when I see it
I always stare anew, because that a poor boat, with the brain
of a man and the hands of a boy on board, can match herself
so bravely against black Heaven and Ocean.

Well, so when you have travelled for days and days over
an Eastern Desert without meeting the likeness of a human
being, and then at last see an Englishman and his servant
come listlessly slouching along from out the forward horizon,
you stare at the wide unproportion between this slender
company and the boundless plains of sand through which they
are keeping their way.

A. W. KINGLAKE, *Eothen.*

### 15.*** THE 'MERRY MEN.'

The night, though we were so little past midsummer, was
as dark as January. Intervals of a groping twilight alternated
with spells of utter blackness; and it was impossible to trace
the reason of these changes in the flying horror of the sky.
The wind blew the breath out of a man's nostrils; all heaven
seemed to thunder overhead like one huge sail; and when
there fell a momentary lull on Aros, we could hear the gusts
dismally sweeping in the distance.

Over all the lowlands of the Ross, the wind must have
blown as fierce as on the open sea; and God only knows the
uproar that was raging around the head of Ben Kyaw. Sheets
of mingled spray and rain were driven in our faces. All
round the isle of Aros the surf, with an incessant, hammering
thunder, beat upon the reefs and beaches. Now louder in one
place, now lower in another, like the combinations of orchestral
music, the constant mass of sound was hardly varied for a
moment. And loud above all this hurly-burly I could hear
the changeful voices of the Roost and the intermittent roaring
of the Merry Men.

At that hour, there flashed into my mind the reason of the
name that they were called. For the noise of them seemed

almost mirthful, as it out-topped the other noises of the night;
or if not mirthful, yet instinct with a portentous joviality.
Nay, and it seemed even human. As when savage men have
drunk away their reason, and, discarding speech, bawl together
in their madness by the hour; so, to my ears, these deadly
breakers shouted by Aros in the night.

R. L. STEVENSON, *The Merry Men.*


### 16.** THE STORM AT YARMOUTH.

The tremendous sea itself, when I could find sufficient pause
to look at it, in the agitation of the blinding wind, the flying
stones and sand, and the awful noise, confounded me.

As the high watery walls came rolling in, and, at their
highest, tumbled into surf, they looked as if the least would
engulf the town. As the receding wave swept back with a
hoarse roar, it seemed to scoop out deep caves in the beach,
as if its purpose were to undermine the earth. When some
white-headed billows thundered on, and dashed themselves to
pieces before they reached the land, every fragment of the late
whole seemed possessed by the full might of its wrath, rushing
to be gathered to the composition of another monster. Undulating hills were changed to valleys, undulating valleys (with
a solitary storm-bird sometimes skimming through them)
were lifted up to hills; masses of water shivered and shook
the beach with a booming sound; every shape tumultuously
rolled on, as soon as made, to change its shape and place, and
beat another shape and place away; the ideal shore on the
horizon, with its towers and buildings, rose and fell; the clouds
flew fast and thick; I seemed to see a rending and upheaving
of all nature.

CHARLES DICKENS, *David Copperfield.*


### 17.** THE SHIPWRECK AT YARMOUTH.

In the difficulty of hearing anything but wind and waves,
and in the crowd, and the unspeakable confusion, and my
first breathless efforts to stand against the weather, I was so

confused that I looked out to sea for the wreck, and saw
nothing but the foaming heads of the great waves. A half-
dressed boatman, standing next me, pointed with his bare
arm (a tattoo'd arrow on it, pointing in the same direction) to
the left. Then, O great Heaven, I saw it, close in upon us!

One mast was broken short off, six or eight feet from the
deck, and lay over the side, entangled in a maze of sail and
rigging; and all that ruin, as the ship rolled and beat—which
she did without a moment's pause, and with a violence quite
inconceivable—beat the side as if it would stave it in. Some
efforts were even then being made to cut this portion of the
wreck away; for, as the ship, which was broadside on, turned
towards us in her rolling, I plainly descried her people at
work with axes, especially one active figure with long curling
hair, conspicuous among the rest. But a great cry, which was
audible even above the wind and water, rose from the shore
at this moment; the sea, sweeping over the rolling wreck,
made a clean breach, and carried men, spars, casks, planks,
bulwarks, heaps of such toys, into the boiling surge.

CHARLES DICKENS, David Copperfield.

## 18.** THE CHASE.

In vain they had strained their eyes through the darkness,
to catch, by the fitful glare of the flashes, the tall masts of the
Spaniard. Of one thing at least they were certain, that with
the wind as it was, she could not have gone far to the westward; and to attempt to pass them again, and go northward,
was more than she dare do. She was probably lying-to ahead
of them, perhaps between them and the land; and when,
a little after midnight, the wind chopped up to the west, and
blew stiffly till daybreak, they felt sure that, unless she had
attempted the desperate expedient of running past them, they
had her safe in the mouth of the Bristol Channel.

Slowly and wearily broke the dawn, on such a day as often
follows heavy thunder; a sunless, drizzly day, roofed with low
dingy cloud, barred and netted, and festooned with black,
a sign that the storm is only taking breath awhile before it

bursts again; while all the narrow horizon is dim and spongy with vapour drifting before a chilly breeze.

As the day went on, the breeze died down, and the sea fell to a long glassy foam-flecked roll, while overhead brooded the inky sky, and round them the leaden mist shut out alike the shore and the chase.

CHARLES KINGSLEY, *Westward Ho!*

### 19.* DR JOHNSON IN SKYE.

We went forward, winding among mountains, sometimes green and sometimes naked, commonly so steep as not to be easily climbed by the greatest vigour and activity; our way was often crossed by little rivulets, and we were entertained with small streams trickling from the rocks, which after heavy rains must be tremendous torrents.

About noon we came to a small glen, so they call a valley, which compared with other places appeared rich and fertile; here our guides desired us to stop, that the horses might graze, for the journey was very laborious, and no more grass would be found. We made no difficulty of compliance, and I sat down to take notes on a green bank, with a small stream running at my feet, in the midst of savage solitude, with mountains before me, and on either hand covered with heath.

I looked around me, and wondered that I was not more affected, but the mind is not at all times equally ready to be put in motion; if my mistress and master and Queeny had been there we should have produced some reflections among us, either poetical or philosophical, for though *solitude be the nurse of woe,* conversation is often the parent of remarks and discoveries.

SAMUEL JOHNSON,
*Letter to Mrs Thrale,* Skye, 21 Sept. 1773.

### 20.** THE OVERTAXED IMAGINATION.

I well recollect the walk on which I first found out this; it was on the winding road from Sallenche, sloping up the hill towards St Gervais, one cloudless Sunday afternoon.

The road circles softly between bits of rocky bank and mounded pasture; little cottages and chapels gleaming out from among the trees at every turn. Behind me, some leagues in length, rose the jagged range of the mountains of the Reposoir; on the other side of the valley, the mass of the Aiguille de Varens, heaving its seven thousand feet of cliff into the air at a single effort, its gentle gift of waterfall, the Nant d'Arpenaz, like a pillar of cloud at its feet; Mont Blanc and all its aiguilles, one silver flame, in front of me; marvellous blocks of mossy granite and dark glades of pine around me; but I could enjoy nothing, and could not for a long while make out what was the matter with me, until at last I discovered that if I confined myself to one thing,—and that a little thing,—a tuft of moss or a single crag at the top of the Varens, or a wreath or two of foam at the bottom of the Nant d'Arpenaz, I began to enjoy it directly, because then I had mind to put into the thing, and the enjoyment arose from the quantity of the imaginative energy I could bring to bear upon it; but when I looked at or thought of all together, moss, stones, Varens, Nant d'Arpenaz, and Mont Blanc, I had not mind enough to give to all, and none were of any value.

JOHN RUSKIN, *Modern Painters*, Vol. III.


### 21.* EASTER DAY IN THE HILLS.

I thought that it was a Sunday morning in May, that it was Easter Sunday, and as yet very early in the morning. I was standing, as it seemed to me, at the door of my own cottage. Right before me lay the very scene which could really be commanded from that situation, but exalted, as was usual, and solemnized by the power of dreams. There were the same mountains, and the same lovely valley at their feet; but the mountains were raised to more than Alpine height, and there was interspace far larger between them of meadows and forest lawns; the hedges were rich with white roses; and no living creature was to be seen, excepting that in the green churchyard there were cattle tranquilly reposing upon the verdant graves,

and particularly round about the grave of a child whom I had
tenderly loved, just as I had really beheld them, a little before
sunrise, in the same summer when that child died.

THOMAS DE QUINCEY,
*Confessions of an English Opium-Eater.*

### 22.* SUMMER IN PORTUGAL.

The day was intensely hot, notwithstanding the coldness of
the preceding nights, and the brilliant sun of Portugal now
illumined a landscape of entrancing beauty. Groves of cork
trees covered the farther side of the valley and the distant
acclivities, exhibiting here and there charming vistas, where
various flocks of cattle were feeding; the soft murmur of the
stream, which was at intervals chafed and broken by huge
stones, ascended to my ears and filled my mind with delicious
feelings. I sat down on the broken wall and remained gazing
and listening and shedding tears of rapture; for of all the
pleasures which a bountiful God permitteth his children to
enjoy, none are so dear to some hearts as the music of forests
and streams, and the view of the beauties of his glorious
creation.

GEORGE BORROW, *The Bible in Spain.*

### 23.** COLOUR IN LANDSCAPE.

The sun came out as I left the shelter of a pine-wood, and
I beheld suddenly a fine wild landscape to the south. High
rocky hills, as blue as sapphire, closed the view, and between
these lay ridge upon ridge, heathery, craggy, the sun glittering
on veins of rock, the underwood clambering in the hollows, as
rude as God made them at the first. There was not a sign of
man's hand in all the prospect; and indeed not a trace of his
passage, save where generation after generation had walked in
twisted footpaths, in and out among the beeches, and up and
down upon the channelled slopes. The mists, which had
hitherto beset me, were now broken into clouds, and fled swiftly
and shone brightly in the sun. I drew a long breath. It was

grateful to come, after so long, upon a scene of some attraction
for the human heart. I own I like definite form in what my
eyes are to rest upon; and if landscapes were sold, like the
sheets of characters of my boyhood, one penny plain and twopence coloured, I should go the length of twopence every day
of my life.

R. L. Stevenson, *Travels with a Donkey.*

### 24.*** Sweet Bells.

On the other side of the valley a group of red roofs and a
belfry showed among the foliage. Thence some inspired bell-
ringer made the afternoon musical on a chime of bells. There
was something very sweet and taking in the air he played; and
we thought we had never heard bells speak so intelligibly or
sing so melodiously as these. It must have been to some such
measure that the spinners and the young maids sang, 'Come
away, Death,' in the Shakespearian Illyria. There is so often
a threatening note, something blatant and metallic, in the voice
of bells, that I believe we have fully more pain than pleasure
from hearing them; but these, as they sounded abroad, now
high, now low, now with a plaintive cadence that caught the
ear like the burthen of a popular song, were always moderate
and tunable, and seemed to fall in with the spirit of still, rustic
places, like the noise of a waterfall or the babble of a rookery
in spring.

I could have asked the bell-ringer for his blessing, good,
sedate old man, who swung the rope so gently to the time of
his meditations.

R. L. Stevenson, *An Inland Voyage.*

### 25.* The Spell of Music.

I remember once strolling along the margin of a stream,
skirted with willows and plashy sedges, in one of those low
sheltered valleys on Salisbury Plain, where the monks of former
ages had planted chapels and built hermits' cells. There was
a little parish church near, but tall elms and quivering alders

hid it from my sight, when, all of a sudden, I was startled by
the sound of the full organ pealing on the ear, accompanied
by rustic voices and the willing quire of village maidens and
children. It rose, indeed, "like an exhalation of rich distilled
perfumes." The dew from a thousand pastures was gathered
in its softness; the silence of a thousand years spoke in it. It
came upon the heart like the calm beauty of death; fancy
caught at the sound, and faith mounted on it to the skies. It
filled the valley like a mist, and still poured out its endless
chant, and still it swells upon the ear, and wraps me in golden
trance, drowning the noisy tumult of the world!

WILLIAM HAZLITT, *Table Talk.*


## 26.* A SUMMER SCENE.

One beautiful June day the doctor and the boy sat upon the
hill outside the village. The river, as blue as heaven, shone
here and there among the foliage. The indefatigable birds
turned and flickered about Gretz church tower. A healthy
wind blew from over the forest, and the sound of innumerable
thousands of tree-tops and innumerable millions on millions of
green leaves was abroad in the air, and filled the ear with
something between whispered speech and singing. It seemed
as if every blade of grass must hide a cigale; and the fields
rang merrily with their music, jingling far and near as with the
sleigh-bells of the fairy queen.

From their station on the slope the eye embraced a large
space of poplar'd plain upon the one hand, the waving hill-tops
of the forest upon the other, and Gretz itself in the middle, a
handful of roofs. Under the bestriding arch of the blue heavens,
the place seemed dwindled to a toy. It seemed incredible that
people dwelt, and could find room to turn or air to breathe, in
such a corner of the world.

R. L. STEVENSON, *The Treasure of Franchard.*

## 27.*** THE BONFIRE.

While the men and lads were building the pile, a change took place in the mass of shade which denoted the distant landscape. Red suns and tufts of fire one by one began to arise, flecking the whole country round. They were the bonfires of other parishes and hamlets that were engaged in the same sort of commemoration. Some were distant, and stood in a dense atmosphere, so that bundles of pale strawlike beams radiated around them in the shape of a fan. Some were large and near, glowing scarlet-red from the shade, like wounds in a black hide. Some were Maenades, with winy faces and blown hair. These tinctured the silent bosom of the clouds above them and lit up their ephemeral caves, which seemed thenceforth to become scalding cauldrons.

Perhaps as many as thirty bonfires could be counted within the whole bounds of the district; and as the hour may be told on a clock-face when the figures themselves are invisible, so did the men recognize the locality of each fire by its angle and direction, though nothing of the scenery could be viewed.

THOMAS HARDY, *The Return of the Native.*

## 28.* AN AUTUMN SCENE.

It was one market-day—Jael being absent—that I came down-stairs. A soft, bright, autumn morning, mild as spring, coaxing a wandering robin to come and sing to me, loud as a quire of birds, out of the thinned trees of the Abbey-yard. I opened the window to hear him, though all the while in mortal fear of Jael. I listened, but caught no tone of her sharp voice, which usually came painfully from the back regions of the house; it would ill have harmonised with the sweet autumn day and the robin's song. I sat, idly thinking so, and wondering whether it were a necessary and universal fact that human beings, unlike the year, should become harsh and unlovely as they grow old.

My robin had done singing and I amused myself with

watching a spot of scarlet, winding down the rural road . . .
It turned out to be the cloak of a well-to-do young farmer's
wife riding to market in her cart beside her jolly-looking spouse.
Very spruce and self-satisfied she appeared, and the market-
people turned to stare after her, for her costume was a novelty
then. Doubtless, many thought as I did, how much prettier
was scarlet than duffle gray.

Mrs CRAIK, *John Halifax, Gentleman.*

### 29.** THE ENGLISH CLIMATE.

Vituperation of the English climate is foolish. A better climate does not exist—for healthy people....In its freedom from
extremes, in its common clemency, even in its caprice, which
at the worst time holds out hope, our island weather compares
well with that of other lands. Who enjoys the fine day of
spring, summer, autumn or winter so much as an Englishman?
His perpetual talk of the weather is testimony to his keen
relish for most of what it offers him: in lands of blue monotony,
even as where climatic conditions are plainly evil, such talk
does not go on. So, granting that we have bad days not a few,
that the east wind takes us by the throat, that the mists get
at our joints, that the sun hides his glory too often and too
long, it is plain that the result of all comes to good, that it en-
genders a mood of zest under the most various aspects of
heaven, keeps an edge on our appetite for open-air life.

GEORGE GISSING, *The Private Papers of Henry Ryecroft.*

### 30.* THE ENGLISH COUNTRYSIDE.

There is no countryside like the English countryside for
those who have learned to love it; its firm yet gentle lines of
hill and dale, its ordered confusion of features, its deer parks
and downland, its castles and stately houses, its hamlets and
old churches, its farms and ricks and great barns and ancient
trees, its pools and ponds and shining threads of rivers, its
flower-starred hedgerows, its orchards and woodland patches,
its village greens and kindly inns.

Other countrysides have their pleasant aspects, but none such variety, none that shine so steadfastly throughout the year. Picardy is pink and white and pleasant in the blossom time; Burgundy goes on with its sunshine and wide hillsides and cramped vineyards, a beautiful tune repeated and repeated; Italy gives salitas and wayside chapels, and chestnuts and olive orchards; the Ardennes has its woods and gorges— Touraine and the Rhineland, the wide Campagna with its distant Apennines, and the neat prosperity and mountain backgrounds of South Germany all clamour their especial merits at one's memory. And there are the hills and fields of Virginia, like an England grown very big and slovenly, the woods and big river sweeps of Pennsylvania, the trim New England landscape, a little bleak and rather fine, like the New England mind, and the wide rough country roads and hills and woodland of New York State.

But none of these change scene and character in three miles of walking, nor have so mellow a sunlight nor so diversified a cloudland nor confess the perpetual refreshment of the strong soft winds that blow from off the sea, as our mother England does. H. G. WELLS, *The History of Mr Polly.*

### 31.*** TWO COTTAGES.

No contrast can be more painful than that between the dwelling of any well-conducted English cottager, and that of the equally honest Savoyard.

The one, set in the midst of its dull flat fields and uninteresting hedgerows, shows in itself the love of brightness and beauty; its daisy-studded garden-beds, its smoothly swept brick path to the threshold, its freshly sanded floor and orderly shelves of household furniture, all testify to energy of heart, and happiness in the simple course and simple possessions of daily life.

The other cottage, in the midst of an inconceivable, inexpressible beauty, set on some sloping bank of golden sward, with clear fountains flowing beside it, and wild-flowers, and noble trees, and goodly rocks gathered round into a perfection

2—2

as of Paradise, is itself a dark and plague-like stain in the midst of the gentle landscape. Within a certain distance of its threshold the ground is foul and cattle-trampled; its timbers are black with smoke, its garden choked with weeds and nameless refuse, its chambers empty and joyless, the light and wind gleaming and filtering through the crannies of their stones.

All testifies that to its inhabitant the world is labour and vanity; that for him neither flowers bloom, nor birds sing, nor fountains glisten; and that his soul hardly differs from the grey cloud that coils and dies upon his hills, except in having no fold of it touched by the sunbeams.

JOHN RUSKIN, Modern Painters, Vol. IV.

### 32.*** THE BLACK COUNTRY.

A dense cloud of pestilential smoke hangs over it for ever, blackening even the grain that grows upon it; and at night the whole region burns like a volcano spitting fire from a thousand tubes of brick.

But, oh, the wretched hundred and fifty thousand mortals that grind out their destiny there! In the coal mines they are literally naked, many of them, all but trousers; black as ravens, plashing about among dripping caverns, or scrambling among heaps of broken mineral; and thirsting unquestionably for beer.

In the iron mills it was little better; blast furnaces were roaring like the voice of many whirlwinds all around; the fiery metal was hissing through its moulds or sparkling and spitting under hammers of a monstrous size, which fell like so many little earthquakes. Here they were wheeling charred coals, breaking their iron-stone and tumbling all into their fiery pit; there they were turning and boring cannon with a hideous shrieking noise such as the earth could hardly parallel; and through the whole, half-naked demons pouring with sweat and besmeared with soot were hurrying to and fro in their red nightcaps and sheet-iron breeches, rolling or hammering or squeezing their glowing metal as if it had been wax or dough.

They also had a thirst for ale. Yet on the whole I am told they are very happy; they make forty shillings or more per week, and few of them will work on Mondays.

THOMAS CARLYLE, *Correspondence.*

## 33.** THE DINGLE.

A path turning and returning at acute angles, led down a steep wood-covered slope to the edge of a chasm, where a pool, or resting-place of a torrent, lay far below. A cataract fell in a single sheet into the pool; the pool boiled and bubbled at the base of the fall, but through the greater part of its extent lay calm, deep and black, as if the cataract had plunged through it to an unimaginable depth without disturbing its eternal repose.

At the opposite extremity of the pool, the rocks almost met at their summits, the trees of the opposite banks intermingled their leaves, and another cataract plunged from the pool into a chasm on which the sunbeams never gleamed.

High above, on both sides, the steep woody slopes of the dingle soared into the sky; and from a fissure in the rock, on which the little path terminated, a single gnarled and twisted oak stretched itself over the pool, forming a fork with its boughs at a short distance from the rock.

T. L. PEACOCK, *Crotchet Castle.*

## 34.*** THE INTRICACY OF NATURE'S FOLIAGE.

But if nature is so various when you have a bough on the table before you, what must she be when she retires from you, and gives you her whole mass and multitude? The leaves then at the extremities become as fine as dust, a mere confusion of points and lines between you and the sky, a confusion which, you might as well hope to draw sea-sand particle by particle, as to imitate leaf for leaf. This, as it comes down into the body of the tree, gets closer, but never opaque; it is always transparent with crumbling lights in it letting you through to the sky: then out of this, come, heavier and heavier, the masses of illumined foliage, all dazzling and inextricable, save here and there a single leaf on the extremities: then, under these, you get deep passages of broken irregular gloom, passing into transparent, green-lighted, misty hollows; the twisted stems glancing through them in their pale and entangled infinity, and the shafted sunbeams, rained from above, running along the lustrous leaves for an instant; then lost, then caught again on some emerald bank or knotted root, to be sent up again with a faint reflex on the white under-sides of dim groups of drooping foliage, the shadows of the upper boughs running in grey network down the glossy stems, and resting in quiet chequers upon the glittering earth; but all penetrable and transparent, and, in proportion, inextricable and incomprehensible, except where across the labyrinth and the mystery of the dazzling light and dream-like shadow, falls, close to us, some solitary spray, some wreath of two or three motionless large leaves, the type and embodying of all that in the rest we feel and imagine, but can never see.

JOHN RUSKIN, *Modern Painters*, Vol. I.

## 35.** GRASS.

Gather a single blade of grass, and examine for a minute, quietly, its narrow sword-shaped strip of fluted green. Nothing, as it seems, there of notable goodness or beauty. A very little strength, and a very little tallness, and a few delicate long lines meeting in a point, not a perfect point neither, but blunt and unfinished, by no means a creditable or apparently much cared for example of Nature's workmanship, made, as it seems, only to be trodden on to-day, and to-morrow to be cast into the oven; and a little pale and hollow stalk, feeble and flaccid, leading down to the dull brown fibres of roots.

And yet, think of it well, and judge whether of all the gorgeous flowers that beam in summer air, and of all strong and goodly trees, pleasant to the eyes or good for food— stately palm and pine, strong ash and oak, scented citron, burdened vine—there be any by man so deeply loved, by God so highly graced, as that narrow point of feeble green.

JOHN RUSKIN, *Modern Painters*, Vol. V.

### 36.**** MONTE MOTTERONE.

The storm has beaten at these peaks until they have got the aspect of the storm. They take colour from sunlight, and are joyless in colour as in shade. When the lower world is under pushing steam, they wear the look of the revolted sons of Time, fast chained before scornful heaven in an iron peace. Day at last brings vigorous fire; arrows of light pierce the mist-wreaths, the dancing draperies, the floors of vapour; and the mountain of piled pasturages is seen with its foot on the shore of Lago Maggiore. Down an extreme gulf the full sunlight, as if darting on a jewel in the deeps, seizes the blue-green lake with its isles. The villages along the darkly-wooded borders of the lake show white as clustered swans; here and there a tented boat is visible, shooting from terraces of vines, or hanging on its shadow.

GEORGE MEREDITH, *Vittoria.*


### 37.*** ABOVE THE VILLAGE OF CHAMPAGNOLE (JURA).

It is a spot which has all the solemnity, with none of the savageness, of the Alps; where there is a sense of a great power beginning to be manifested in the earth, and of a deep and majestic concord in the rise of the long low lines of piny hills; the first utterance of those mighty mountain symphonies, soon to be more loudly lifted and wildly broken along the battlements of the Alps.

But their strength is as yet restrained; and the far reaching ridges of pastoral mountain succeed each other, like the long and sighing swell which moves over quiet waters from some far-off stormy sea.

And there is a deep tenderness pervading that vast monotony. The destructive forces and the stern expression of the central ranges are alike withdrawn. No frost-ploughed, dust-encumbered paths of ancient glacier fret the soft Jura pastures; no splintered heaps of ruin break the fair ranks of her forest; no pale, defiled, or furious rivers rend their rude and changeful ways among her rocks. Patiently, eddy by eddy, the clear green streams wind along their well-known beds; and under the dark quietness of the undisturbed pines, there spring up, year by year, such company of joyful flowers as I know not the like of among all the blessings of the earth.

JOHN RUSKIN, *The Seven Lamps of Architecture.*

## 38.** THE APPROACH TO VENICE.

In the olden days of travelling, there were few moments of which the recollection was more fondly cherished by the traveller than that, which brought him within sight of Venice, as his gondola shot into the open lagoon from the canal of Mestre.

Not but that the aspect of the city itself was generally the source of some slight disappointment, for, seen in this direction, its buildings are far less characteristic than those of the other great towns of Italy; but this inferiority was partly disguised by distance, and more than atoned for by the strange rising of its walls and towers out of the midst, as it seemed, of the deep sea, for it was impossible that the mind or the eye could at once comprehend the shallowness of the vast sheet of water which stretched away in leagues of rippling lustre to the north and south, or trace the narrow line of islets bounding it to the east.

The salt breeze, the white moaning sea-birds, the masses of black weed separating and disappearing gradually, in knots of heaving shoal, under the advance of the steady tide, all proclaimed it to be indeed the ocean on whose bosom the great city rested so calmly; not such blue, soft, lake-like ocean as bathes the Neapolitan promontories, or sleeps beneath the marble rocks of Genoa, but a sea with the bleak power of our own northern waves, yet subdued into a strange spacious rest, and changed from its angry pallor into a field of burnished gold, as the sun declined behind the belfry of the lonely island church, fitly named "St George of the Sea-weed."

JOHN RUSKIN, *The Stones of Venice.*

## 39.** THE ARICIAN GROVE.

Who does not know Turner's picture of the Golden Bough? The scene, suffused with the golden glow of imagination in which the divine mind of Turner steeped and transfigured even the fairest natural landscape, is a dream-like vision of the little woodland lake of Nemi, "Diana's Mirror," as it was called by the ancients. No one who has seen that calm water, lapped in a green hollow of the Alban Hills, can ever forget it. The two characteristic Italian villages which slumber on its banks, and the equally Italian palace whose terraced gardens descend steeply to the lake, hardly break the stillness, and even the solitariness, of the scene. Diana herself might still linger by this lonely shore, still haunt these woodlands wild.

In antiquity this sylvan landscape was the scene of a strange and recurring tragedy. On the northern shore of the lake, right under the precipitous cliffs on which the modern village of Nemi is perched, stood the sacred grove and sanctuary of Diana Nemorensis, or Diana of the Wood. The lake and the grove were sometimes known as the lake and grove of Aricia. But the town of Aricia (the modern La Riccia) was situated about three miles off, at the foot of the Alban Mount, and separated by a steep descent from the lake, which lies in a small crater-like hollow on the mountain side.

In this sacred grove there grew a certain tree round which at any time of the day, and probably far into the night, a grim figure might be seen to prowl. In his hand he carried a drawn sword, and he kept peering warily about him as if every instant he expected to be set upon by an enemy. He was a priest and a murderer; and the man for whom he looked was sooner or later to murder him and hold the priesthood in his stead. Such was the rule of the sanctuary. A candidate for the priesthood could only succeed to office by slaying the priest, and having slain him, he retained office till he was himself slain by a stronger or a craftier.

Sir JAMES G. FRAZER, *The Golden Bough.*

### 40.** The Arician Grove (*continued*).

The post which he held by this precarious tenure carried with it the title of king; but surely no crowned head ever lay uneasier, or was visited by more evil dreams, than his. For year in year out, in summer and winter, in fair weather and in foul, he had to keep his lonely watch, and whenever he snatched a troubled slumber it was at the peril of his life. The least relaxation of his vigilance, the smallest abatement of his strength of limb or skill of fence, put him in jeopardy; gray hairs might seal his death-warrant.

To gentle and pious pilgrims at the shrine the sight of him may well have appeared to darken the fair landscape, as when a cloud suddenly blots the sun on a bright day. The dreamy blue of Italian skies, the dappled shade of summer woods, and the sparkle of waves in the sun can have accorded but ill with that stern and sinister figure. Rather we picture to ourselves the scene as it may have been witnessed by a belated wayfarer on one of those wild autumn nights when the dead leaves are falling thick, and the winds seem to sing the dirge of the dying year.

It is a sombre picture set to melancholy music—the background of forest showing black and jagged against a lowering and stormy sky, the sighing of the wind in the branches, the rustle of the withered leaves under foot, the lapping of the cold water on the shore, and in the foreground, pacing to and fro, now in twilight and now in gloom, a dark figure with a glitter as of steel at the shoulder whenever the pale moon, riding clear of the cloud-rack, peers down at him through the matted boughs.

Sir James G. Frazer, *The Golden Bough.*

### 41.* The Pass of Glencoe.

In the Gaelic tongue, Glencoe signifies the Glen of Weeping: and in truth that pass is the most dreary and melancholy of all the Scottish passes, the very Valley of the Shadow of Death. Mists and storms brood over it through the greater part of the finest summer; and even on those rare days when the sun is bright, and when there is no cloud in the sky, the impression made by the landscape is sad and awful.

The path lies along a stream which issues from the most sullen and gloomy of mountain pools. Huge precipices of naked stone frown on both sides. Even in July the streaks of snow may often be discerned in the rifts near the summits. All down the sides of the crags heaps of ruin mark the headlong paths of the torrents. Mile after mile the traveller looks in vain for the smoke of one hut, or for one human form wrapped in a plaid, and listens in vain for the bark of a shepherd's dog, or the bleat of a lamb. Mile after mile the only sound that indicates life is the faint cry of a bird of prey from some storm-beaten pinnacle of rock.

The progress of civilisation, which has turned so many wastes into fields yellow with harvests or gay with apple blossoms, has only made Glencoe more desolate. All the science and industry of a peaceful age can extract nothing valuable from that wilderness: but, in an age of violence and rapine, the wilderness itself was valued on account of the shelter which it afforded to the plunderer and his plunder.

Lord MACAULAY, History of England.

## 42.** THE FLOSS.

A wide plain, where the broadening Floss hurries on between its green banks to the sea, and the loving tide, rushing to meet it, checks its passage with an impetuous embrace. On this mighty tide the black ships—laden with the fresh-scented fir-planks, with rounded sacks of oil-bearing seed, or with the dark glitter of coal,—are borne along to the town of St Ogg's, which shows its aged, fluted red roofs and the broad gables of its wharves between the low wooded hill and the river brink, tinging the water with a soft purple hue under the transient glance of this February sun.

Far away on each hand stretch the rich pastures, and the patches of dark earth, made ready for the seed of broad-leaved green crops, or touched already with the tint of the tender-bladed autumn-sown corn. There is a remnant still of the last year's golden clusters of beehive ricks rising at intervals beyond the hedgerows; and everywhere the hedgerows are studded with trees; the distant ships seem to be lifting their masts and stretching their red-brown sails close among the branches of the spreading ash.

GEORGE ELIOT, *The Mill on the Floss.*

### 43.* YARROW.

In such manner did life pass by in the grey stone dwelling which crowned the Yarrow braes, with Yarrow crooning in the nooks below. It was but yesterday I passed the place, which no lapse of years can change. The vale of long green hills which falls eastward from the lochs is treeless and desert for miles, with a wan stream sweeping 'neath barren hill-shoulders and the grey-green bent lending melancholy to all. But of a sudden it changes to a defile; the hills huddle together till the waters can scarce find passage; and a forest of wildwood chokes the gorge. Brown heather and green hazels crest every scarred rock and fringe the foot of Birkenshaw Tower, which looks steeply down on its woodland valley. Soft meadow-grass is shaded by a tangle of ashes, and in every dell the burn's trickle slips through a wild flower-garden; while in broad pools and shining stretches Yarrow goes singing her ageless song for evermore.

JOHN BUCHAN, *A Lost Lady of Old Years.*

### 44.** LONDON.

The view from the bridge over the Serpentine has an extra-ordinary nobleness, and it has often seemed to me that the Londoner twitted with his low standard may point to it with every confidence. In all the town-scenery of Europe there can be few things so fine, the only reproach it is open to is that it begs the question by seeming—in spite of its being the pride of five millions of people—not to belong to a town at all. The towers of Notre-Dame, as they rise, in Paris, from the island that divides the Seine, present themselves no more impressively than those of Westminster as you see them looking doubly far beyond the shining stretch of Hyde Park water. Equally admirable is the large, river-like manner in which the Serpentine opens away between its wooded shores.

Just after you have crossed the bridge (whose very banisters, old and ornamental, of yellowish-brown stone, I am particularly fond of), you enjoy on your left, through the gate of Kensington Gardens as you go towards Bayswater, an altogether enchanting vista—a foot-path over the grass, which loses itself beneath the scattered oaks and elms exactly as if the place were a "chase." There could be nothing less like London in general than this particular morsel, and yet it takes London of all cities, to give you such an impression of the country.

HENRY JAMES, *Essays in London and Elsewhere.*

### 45.* SYDNEY.

I walked up in the twilight to the esplanade at the gate of the public garden, and I think I have never in my life gazed on a scene so entirely beautiful.

The ground slopes from the town to the sea with inclining lawns, flower-beds, and the endless variety of the tropical flora. Tall Norfolk Island pines tower up dark into the air, and grand walks wind for miles among continually varying landscapes, which are framed by the openings in the foliage of the perfumed shrubs.

Within the compass of the garden the sea forms two deep bays, one of which is reserved for the ships of the squadron. Five vessels lay at anchor there, their spars black against the evening sky, and the long pennants drooping at the masthead; the 'Nelson' sitting like a queen in the midst of them, the admiral's white flag hanging over the stern. Steam-launches were gliding at half power over the glassy waters, which were pink with the reflection of the sunset. Boats were bringing off officers and men who had been at leave on shore; the old order, form, and discipline in the new land of liberty—the shield behind which alone the vaunted liberty is possible.

Behind the anchorage were rocky islands, with the deserted ruins of ancient batteries, now useless and superseded by ampler fortifications inside the bluffs. Merchant ships lay scattered over the outer harbour, and a yacht or two lay drifting with idle sails. Crowded steam ferry-boats were carrying the workmen home from the city to distant villages.

J. A. FROUDE, *Oceana.*

### 46.*** CHICAGO.

Suddenly the meaning and significance of it all dawned upon Laura. The Great Grey City, brooking no rival, imposed its dominion upon a reach of country larger than many a kingdom of the Old World.

For thousands of miles beyond its confines was its influence felt. Out, far out, far away in the snow and shadow of Northern Wisconsin forests, axes and saws bit the bark of century-old trees, stimulated by this city's energy. Just as far to the southward pick and drill leaped to the assault of veins of anthracite, moved by her central power. Her force turned the wheels of harvester and seeder a thousand miles distant in Iowa and Kansas. Her force spun the screws and propellers of innumerable squadrons of lake steamers crowding the Sault Sainte Marie. For her and because of her all the Central States, all the Great North-west roared with traffic and industry; saw-mills screamed; factories, their smoke blackening the sky, clashed and flamed; wheels turned, pistons leaped in their cylinders, cog gripped cog, beltings clasped the drums of mammoth wheels, and converters of forges belched into the clouded air their tempest-breath of molten steel.

It was Empire, the resistless subjugation of all this central world of the lakes and the prairies. Here, midmost in the land, beat the Heart of the Nation, whence inevitably must come its immeasurable power, its infinite, inexhaustible vitality. Here, of all her cities, throbbed the true life—the true power and spirit of America; gigantic, crude with the crudity of youth, disdaining rivalry; sane and healthy and vigorous; brutal in its ambition, arrogant in the new-found knowledge of its giant strength, prodigal of its wealth, infinite in its desires.

FRANK NORRIS, *The Pit.*

## 47.*** HOLYROOD.

The Palace of Holyrood has been left aside in the growth of Edinburgh, and stands grey and silent in a workman's quarter and among breweries and gas works. It is a house of many memories. Great people of yore, kings and queens, buffoons and grave ambassadors, played their stately farce for centuries in Holyrood. Wars have been plotted, dancing has lasted deep into the night, murder has been done in its chambers. There Prince Charlie held his phantom levées, and in a very gallant manner represented a fallen dynasty for some hours. Now, all these things of clay are mingled with the dust; the king's crown itself is shown for sixpence to the vulgar; but the stone palace has outlived these changes.

For fifty weeks together it is no more than a show for tourists and a museum of old furniture; but on the fifty-first, behold the palace reawakened and mimicking its past. The Lord Commissioner, a kind of stage sovereign, sits among stage courtiers; a coach and six and clattering escort come and go before the gate; at night, the windows are lighted up, and its near neighbours, the workmen, may dance in their own houses to the palace music.

And in this the palace is typical. There is a spark among the embers; from time to time the old volcano smokes. Edinburgh has but partly abdicated, and still wears, in parody, her metropolitan trappings. Half a capital and half a country town, the whole city leads a double existence; it has long trances of the one and flashes of the other; like the king of the Black Isles, it is half alive and half a monumental marble.

R. L. STEVENSON, *Edinburgh*.

## 48.** TRINITY COLLEGE, CAMBRIDGE.

The windows of my study look on the tranquil court of an ancient college, where the sundial marks the silent passage of the hours and in the long summer days the fountain plashes drowsily amid flowers and grass; where, as the evening shadows deepen, the lights come out in the blazoned windows of the

Elizabethan hall and from the chapel the sweet voices of the choir, blent with the pealing music of the organ, float on the peaceful air, telling of man's eternal aspirations after truth and goodness and immortality.

Here, if anywhere, remote from the tumult and bustle of the world with its pomps and vanities and ambitions, the student may hope to hear the still voice of truth, to penetrate through the little transitory questions of the hour to the realities which abide, or rather which we fondly think must abide, while the generations come and go. I cannot be too thankful that I have been allowed to spend so many quiet and happy years in such a scene, and when I quit my old college rooms as I soon shall do, for another home in Cambridge, I shall hope to carry forward to new work in a new scene the love of study and labour which has been not indeed implanted, but fostered and cherished in this ancient home of learning and peace.

Sir JAMES G. FRAZER, Pausanias.

## 49.**** KING'S COLLEGE, ABERDEEN.

Memory is a musician with whom you cannot call the tune. Ask for a true tale of the past, and you get nothing but snatches of irrelevant lyric. So, when I try to remember what the days were like when the long tradition was broken and women first came to King's, I become lost in a reverie of beautiful inconsequent images. The irregular black houses of the descending Spital, made miraculously strange and solemn by a fresh fall of snow, a flight of birds pulsing across the great virginal-blue sky above the Aulton turrets on a mild Saint Valentine's morning, a shaft of jewelled light striking through the carved places of the Chapel, the dissolving groups of the quadrangle, and the proud poise of some bright head that moves no longer among the living, the joy of hearing for the first time the rushing cadence of Swinburne, thrown out like a golden libation in the quiet class-room, the sense of spiritual adventure in the air, the setting of the untired falcon of the will at impossible quarry—all the irresponsible gaiety and exaggerated pessimism, the bright audacities, the not ignoble follies of youth, ebbing and flowing under that dreaming Crown-tower so compassionately used to the ways of youth,—these are the treasures of remembrance. And, brooding on these, one hardly cares to think if one were with the men or with the women.

Mrs RACHEL ANNAND TAYLOR,<br>
*The Coming of the Women Students.*

50.**** A WRECKED TOWN.

The stillness was as terrible as the spread of the quick busy weeds between the paving-stones; the air smelt of pounded mortar and crushed stone; the sound of a footfall echoed like the drop of a pebble in a well. At first the horror of wrecked apartment-houses and big shops laid open makes one waste energy in anger. It is not seemly that rooms should be torn out of the sides of buildings as one tears the soft heart out of English bread; that villa roofs should lie across iron gates of private garages, or that drawing-room doors should flap alone and disconnected between two emptinesses of twisted girders. The eye wearies of the repeated pattern that burst shells make on stone walls, as the mouth sickens of the taste of mortar and charred timber. One quarter of the place had been shelled nearly level; the façades of the houses stood doorless, roofless, and windowless like stage scenery. This was near the cathedral, which is always a favourite mark for the heathen. They had gashed and ripped the sides of the cathedral itself, so that the birds flew in and out at will; they had smashed holes in the roof; knocked huge cantles out of the buttresses, and pitted and starred the paved square outside.

RUDYARD KIPLING, *France at War.*

51.* EN PROVINCE.

The long warm summers and the pleasant surroundings of a rural French town have aided in the formation of these habits. There are the avenues to walk under—fine avenues of elm, or linden, or oriental plane-tree, the green seats to rest upon and talk, the *cafés* close by, with their tables and chairs outside on the broad *trottoir*, the club-rooms upstairs, with their open windows and balconies, from which you have perhaps a view of hill or wood, or winding river.

Then there is nothing particularly disagreeable in the little town itself—no coal-smoke, no rows of especially ugly houses, but the old streets are quaintly picturesque, and the new boulevard is bright and gay, so that one can walk pleasantly anywhere.

And the country is so near all round! In a quarter of an hour you have passed the old walls, and are in it, amongst the gardens.

There are gardens, too, in the heart of the little city itself; the doctor walks in his garden, and plucks a peach, between the visits of two patients; the banker's counting-house is in his garden, and he walks about amongst his flowers, which refresh his mind with other thoughts than that eternal money.

P. G. HAMERTON, Round My House.

### 52.* AT LONGWOOD.

The lord of so many palaces, who had slept as a conqueror in so many palaces not his own, was now confined to two small rooms of equal size—about fourteen feet by twelve, and ten or eleven high. To this little measure had shrunk all his conquests, glories, triumphs, spoils.

Each of these rooms was lit by two small windows looking towards the regimental camp. In one corner was the little camp-bed with green silk curtains, which the Emperor had used at Marengo and Austerlitz. To hide the back door, there was a screen, and between this screen and the fireplace an old sofa, on which Napoleon passed most of his day, though it was so covered with books that there was scarcely room for comfort. The walls were covered with brown nankeen, and amid the general squalor a magnificent wash-hand-stand with silver ewers and basins displayed an uncongenial splendour.

In the second room there were a writing-table, some bookshelves, and another bed, on which the Emperor would rest in the daytime, or to which he would change from the other, when he was, as was generally the case, restless and sleepless at night.

THE EARL OF ROSEBERY, Napoleon: the Last Phase.

### 53.*** THE INTERIOR OF ST MARK'S.

Through the heavy door, whose bronze network closes the tomb, let us enter the church itself. It is lost in still deeper twilight, to which the eye must be accustomed for some moments before the form of the building can be traced; and then there opens before us a vast cave, hewn out into the form of a Cross, and divided into shadowy aisles by many pillars. Round the domes of its roof the light enters only through narrow apertures like large stars; and here and there a ray or two from some far-away casement wanders into the darkness, and casts a narrow phosphoric stream upon the waves of marble that heave and fall in a thousand colours along the floor. What else there is of light is from torches or silver lamps, burning ceaselessly in the recesses of the chapels; the roof sheeted with gold, and the polished walls covered with alabaster give back, at every curve and angle, some feeble gleaming to the flames; and the glories round the heads of the sculptured saints flash out upon us as we pass them, and sink again into the gloom.

JOHN RUSKIN, *The Stones of Venice.*

### 54.* IN A MEDIÆVAL CASTLE.

In the great stone fireplace a log fire was spurting and crackling, throwing out a ruddy glare which, with the four bracket-lamps which stood at each corner of the room, gave a bright and lightsome air to the whole apartment. Above was a wreath-work of blazonry, extending up to the carved and corniced oaken roof; while on either side stood the high canopied chairs placed for the master of the house and for his most honoured guest.

The walls were hung all round with most elaborate and brightly-coloured tapestry representing the achievements of Sir Bevis of Hampton, and behind this convenient screen were stored the tables dormant and benches which would be needed for banquet or high festivity. The floor was of polished tiles,

3—2

with a square of red and black diapered Flemish carpet in
the centre; and many settees, cushions, folding chairs, and
carved bancals littered all over it. At the farther end was a
long black buffet or dresser, thickly covered with gold cups,
silver salvers, and other such valuables.

All this Alleyne examined with curious eyes; but most
interesting of all to him was a small ebony table at his very
side, on which, by the side of a chess-board and the scattered
chessmen, there lay an open manuscript written in a right
clerkly hand, and set forth with brave flourishes and devices
along the margins.

Sir A. CONAN DOYLE, The White Company.

## 55.* AN IRISH SCHOOLBOY'S DREAM.

A voice bade the boys in the dormitory goodnight. Stephen
peered out for an instant over the coverlet and saw the yellow
curtains round and before his bed that shut him off on all
sides. The light was lowered quietly.

The prefect's shoes went away. Where? Down the staircase and along the corridors or to his room at the end? He
saw the dark. Was it true about the black dog that walked
there at night with eyes as big as carriage-lamps? They said
it was the ghost of a murderer. A long shiver of fear flowed
over his body. He saw the dark entrance hall of the castle.
Old servants in old dress were in the ironing-room above the
staircase. It was long ago. The old servants were quiet.
There was a fire there but the hall was still dark. A figure
came up the staircase from the hall. He wore the white cloak
of a marshal; his face was pale and strange; he held his hand
pressed to his side. He looked out of strange eyes at the old
servants. They looked at him and saw their master's face and
cloak and knew that he had received his death-wound. But
only the dark was where they looked : only dark silent air.
Their master had received his death-wound on the battlefield
of Prague far away over the sea. He was standing on the
field ; his hand was pressed to his side ; his face was pale and
strange and he wore the white cloak of a marshal.

O how cold and strange it was to think of that! All the dark was cold and strange. There were pale strange faces there, great eyes like carriage-lamps. They were the ghosts of murderers, the figures of marshals who had received their death-wound on battlefields far away over the sea. What did they wish to say that their faces were so strange?

JAMES JOYCE, *A Portrait of the Artist as a Young Man.*

## 56.** AN IRISH SCHOOLBOY'S DREAM (*continued*).

Going home for the holidays! That would be lovely: the fellows had told him. Getting up on the cars in the early wintry morning outside the door of the castle. The cars were rolling on the gravel. Cheers for the rector!

Hurray! Hurray! Hurray!

The cars drove past the chapel and all caps were raised. They drove merrily along the country roads. The drivers pointed with their whips to Bodenstown. The fellows cheered. They passed the farmhouse of the Jolly Farmer. Cheer after cheer after cheer. Through Clane they drove, cheering and cheered. The peasant women stood at the half-doors, the men stood here and there. The lovely smell there was in the wintry air; the smell of Clane: rain and wintry air and turf smouldering and corduroy.

The train was full of fellows: a long long chocolate train with cream facings. The guards went to and fro opening, closing, locking, unlocking the doors. They were men in dark blue and silver; they had silvery whistles and their keys made a quick music: click, click; click, click.

And the train raced on over the flat lands and past the Hill of Allen. The telegraph-poles were passing, passing. The train went on and on. It knew. There were lanterns in the hall of his father's house and ropes of green branches. There were holly and ivy round the pier-glass and holly and ivy, green and red, twined round the chandeliers. There were red holly and green ivy round the old portraits on the walls. Holly and ivy for him and for Christmas.

Lovely....All the people. Welcome home, Stephen! Noises of welcome. His mother kissed him. Was that right? His father was a marshal now: higher than a magistrate. Welcome home, Stephen!

JAMES JOYCE, *A Portrait of the Artist as a Young Man.*


### 57.** CHRISTMAS.

Fine old Christmas, with the snowy hair and ruddy face, had done his duty that year in the noblest fashion, and had set off his rich gifts of warmth and colour with all the heightening contrast of frost and snow.

Snow lay on the croft and river-bank in undulations softer than the limbs of infancy; it lay with the neatliest finished border on every sloping roof, making the dark-red gables stand out with a new depth of colour; it weighed heavily on the laurels and fir-trees, till it fell from them with a shuddering sound; it clothed the rough turnip-field with whiteness, and made the sheep look like dark blotches; the gates were all blocked up with the sloping drifts, and here and there a dis-regarded four-footed beast stood as if petrified "in unrecum-bent sadness"; there was no gleam, no shadow, for the heavens, too, were one still, pale cloud—no sound or motion in anything but the dark river that flowed and moaned like an unresting sorrow.

GEORGE ELIOT, *The Mill on the Floss.*


### 58.** CHRISTMAS (*continued*).

But old Christmas smiled as he laid this cruel-seeming spell on the outdoor world, for he meant to light up home with new brightness, to deepen all the richness of indoor colour, and give a keener edge of delight to the warm fragrance of food: he meant to prepare a sweet imprisonment that would strengthen the primitive fellowship of kindred, and make the sunshine of familiar human faces as welcome as the hidden day-star.

His kindness fell but hardly on the homeless—fell but hardly on the homes where the hearth was not very warm, and where the food had little fragrance; where the human faces had no sunshine in them, but rather the leaden, blank-eyed gaze of unexpectant want. But the fine old season meant well; and if he has not learnt the secret how to bless men impartially, it is because his father Time, with ever-unrelenting purpose, still hides that secret in his own mighty, slow-beating heart.

GEORGE ELIOT, *The Mill on the Floss.*

### 59.*** A SCOTTISH FUNERAL.

Four stalwart neighbours, holding their hats, which tapped upon their legs, hoisted the coffin to their shoulders and shuffled to the door. They stooped to let their burden pass beneath the eaves which overhung the entrance, and then emerging, dazed, into the light, their black clothes dusted over with the white ashes from the fire, set down the coffin on the cart. Once more the men gathered into a circle and listened to a prayer, some with their heads bare to the rain, and others with their hats held on the slant to fend it off as it came swirling down the blast.

A workman in his ordinary clothes took the tall, white-faced horse close by the bit, and, with a jolt which made the coffin shift up against the backboard, the cart set out, swaying amongst the ruts, with now and then a wheel running up high upon one side and now and then a jerk upon the trace-hooks, when the horse, cold with his long wait, strained wildly on the chains.

The rain had blotted out the hills, the distant village with its rival kirks had disappeared, and the grey sky appeared to touch the surface of the moor. A whitish dew hung on the grass and made the seeded plants appear gigantic in the gloom. Nothing was to be heard except the roaring of the burn and the sharp ringing of the high caulkins of the horse as he struck fire amongst the stones on the steep, rocky road.

Leaning against the doorpost, the widow stood and gazed after the vanishing procession till it had disappeared into the mist, her tears, which she had fought so bravely to keep back, now running down her face.

When the last sound of the cart-wheels and of the horse's feet amongst the stones had vanished into the thick air, she turned away, and, sitting down before the fire, began mechanically to smoor the peats and tidy up the hearth.

R. B. CUNNINGHAME GRAHAM,
*Scottish Stories (At Dalmary).*

## 60.*** RAISING THE 'KEEN.'

Outside the church door, when benediction ended and no one was left in the building but the schoolmaster teaching children their catechism in Irish, a ritual more distinctive still was enacted.

Perhaps fifty out of that immense congregation made their way into the churchyard, and stood for the most part chatting in a group round the monument to a departed priest. But a few women there detached themselves from the rest, and, each of them picking her way through the grass to a grave-stone or the little cross that marked a tomb still simpler, knelt down, and, bending forward, pressed her face close to the ground. Then—from the very earth it seemed—there rose a faint crying, hardly louder at first than a cricket's noise—swelling, dying down, swelling again, yet always so faint that out there in the open it was hardly audible ten yards off, unless one strained to hear it.

But then a woman raised the chant from a grave just beside us; and, as one listened to her cry near at hand, and the other faint wailings, all chanted to the same heart-rending little tune, they seemed to fill all earth and heaven. It was like the cry, not of this or that wife or mother, but of the land itself—a voice issuing here from among the graves—the wailing of Ireland after her scattered sons.

STEPHEN GWYNN,
*For Second Reading: A Sunday in Donegal.*

## II. PORTRAITS

### 61.*** SWINBURNE.

Swinburne's entry was for me a great moment. Here, suddenly visible in the flesh, was the legendary being and divine singer. Here he was, shutting the door behind him, as might anyone else, and advancing—a strange small figure in grey, having an air at once noble and roguish, proud and skittish. My name was roared to him. In shaking his hand, I bowed low, of course—a bow *de cœur*; and he, in the old aristocratic manner, bowed equally low, but with such swiftness that we narrowly escaped concussion.

You do not usually associate a man of genius, when you see one, with any social class; and, Swinburne being of an aspect so unrelated as it was to any species of human kind, I wondered the more that almost the first impression he made on me, or would make on anyone, was that of a very great gentleman indeed. Not of an *old* gentleman, either. Sparse and straggling though the grey hair was that fringed the immense pale dome of his head, and venerably haloed though he was for me by his greatness, there was yet about him something—boyish? girlish? childish, rather; something of a beautifully well-bred child. But he had the eyes of a god, and the smile of an elf.

In figure, at first glance, he seemed almost fat; but this was merely because of the way he carried himself, with his long neck strained so tightly back that he all receded from the waist upwards. I noticed afterwards that this deportment made the back of his jacket hang quite far away from his legs; and so small and sloping were his shoulders that the jacket seemed ever so likely to slip right off. I became aware, too, that when he bowed he did not unbend his back, but only his neck—the length of the neck accounting for the depth of the bow. His hands were tiny, even for his size, and they fluttered helplessly, touchingly, unceasingly.

MAX BEERBOHM, *And Even Now.*

### 62.** WARREN HASTINGS.

The Sergeants made proclamation. Hastings advanced to the bar, and bent his knee. The culprit was indeed not unworthy of that great presence. He had ruled an extensive and populous country, and made laws and treaties, had sent forth armies, had set up and pulled down princes. And in his high place he had so borne himself, that all feared him, that most had loved him, and that hatred itself could deny him no title to glory, except virtue.

He looked like a great man, and not like a bad man. A person small and emaciated, yet deriving dignity from a carriage which, while it indicated deference to the court, indicated also habitual self-possession and self-respect, a high and intellectual forehead, a brow pensive, but not gloomy, a mouth of inflexible decision, a face pale and worn, but serene, on which was written, as legibly as under the picture in the council-chamber at Calcutta, *Mens æqua in arduis*; such was the aspect with which the great proconsul presented himself to his judges.

LORD MACAULAY, *Essays*.

### 63.* FRIDAY.

He was a comely handsome fellow, perfectly well-made, with straight, long limbs, not too large, tall and well-shaped, and, as I reckon, about twenty-six years of age. He had a very good countenance, not a fierce and surly aspect; but seemed to have something very manly in his face; and yet he had all the sweetness and softness of a European in his countenance too, especially when he smiled. His hair was long and black, not curled like wool; his forehead high and large; and a great vivacity and sparkling sharpness in his eyes. The colour of his skin was not quite black, but very tawny; and yet not of an ugly, yellow, nauseous tawny, as the Brazilians and Virginians and other natives of America are, but of a bright kind of dull olive colour, that had in it something very agreeable though not very easy to describe. His face was round and plump, his nose small, not flat like the negroes, a very good mouth, thin lips, and his teeth fine, well-set and white as ivory.

DANIEL DEFOE, *Robinson Crusoe*.

### 64.** Mrs Poyser.

Do not suppose, however, that Mrs Poyser was elderly or shrewish in her appearance; she was a good-looking woman, not more than eight-and-thirty, of fair complexion and sandy hair, well-shapen, light-footed: the most conspicuous article in her attire was an ample checkered linen apron, which almost covered her skirt; and nothing could be plainer or less noticeable than her cap and gown, for there was no weakness of which she was less tolerant than feminine vanity, and the preference of ornament to utility.

The family likeness between her and her niece Dinah Morris, with the contrast between her keenness and Dinah's seraphic gentleness of expression, might have served a painter as an excellent suggestion for Martha and Mary. Their eyes were just of the same colour, but a striking test of the difference in their operation was seen in the demeanour of Trip, the black-and-tan terrier, whenever that much-suspected dog unwarily exposed himself to the freezing arctic ray of Mrs Poyser's glances. Her tongue was not less keen than her eye, and whenever a damsel came within earshot, seemed to take up an unfinished lecture, as a barrel-organ takes up a tune, precisely at the point where it had left off.

GEORGE ELIOT, *Adam Bede.*

### 65.** Eleanor Bold.

A regular service of baby-worship was going on. Mary Bold was sitting on a low easy chair, with the boy in her lap, and Eleanor was kneeling before the object of her idolatry. As she tried to cover up the little fellow's face with her long, glossy, dark brown locks, and permitted him to pull them hither and thither, as he would, she looked very beautiful in spite of the widow's cap which she still wore.

There was a quiet, enduring, grateful sweetness about her face, which grew so strongly upon those who knew her, as to make the great praise of her beauty which came from her old friends, appear marvellously exaggerated to those who were only slightly acquainted with her. Her loveliness was like that of many landscapes, which require to be often seen to be fully enjoyed. There was a depth of dark clear brightness in her eyes which was lost upon a quick observer, a character about her mouth which only showed itself to those with whom she familiarly conversed, a glorious form of head, the perfect symmetry of which required the eye of an artist for its appreciation.

She had none of that dazzling brilliancy, of that voluptuous Rubens beauty, of that pearly whiteness, and those vermilion tints, which immediately entranced with the power of a basilisk men who came within reach of Madeline Neroni. It was all but impossible to resist the Signora, but no one was called upon for any resistance towards Eleanor.

ANTHONY TROLLOPE, *Barchester Towers.*

### 66.**** CLARA MIDDLETON.

She had the mouth that smiles in repose. The lips met full on the centre of the bow and thinned along to a lifting dimple; the eyelids also lifted slightly at the outer corners and seemed, like the lip into the limpid cheek, quickening up the temples, as with a run of light. Her features were playfellows of one another, none of them pretending to rigid correctness, nor the nose to the ordinary dignity of governess among merry girls, despite which the nose was of a fair design, not acutely interrogative or inviting to gambols.

Aspens imaged in water, waiting for the breeze, would offer a susceptible lover some suggestion of her face: a pure smooth-white face, tenderly flushed in the cheeks, where the gentle dints were faintly intermelting even during quietness. Her eyes were brown, set well between mild lids, often shadowed, not unwakeful. Her hair of lighter brown, swelling above her temples on the sweep to the knot, imposed the triangle of the fabulous wild woodland visage from brow to mouth and chin, evidently in agreement with her taste; and the triangle suited her; but her face was not significant of a tameless wildness or of weakness; her equable shut mouth threw its long curve to guard the small round chin from that effect; her eyes wavered only in humour, they were steady when thoughtfulness was awakened; and at such seasons the build of her winter-beechwood hair lost the touch of nymph-like and whimsical, and strangely, by mere outline, added to her appearance of studious concentration.

GEORGE MEREDITH, *The Egoist.*


## 67.** SCROOGE.

Oh! But he was a tight-fisted hand at the grindstone, Scrooge! a squeezing, wrenching, grasping, scraping, clutching, covetous, old sinner! Hard and sharp as flint, from which no steel had ever struck out generous fire; secret and self-contained, and solitary as an oyster. The cold within him froze his old features, nipped his pointed nose, shrivelled his cheek, stiffened his gait; made his eyes red, his thin lips blue; and spoke out shrewdly in his grating voice. A frosty rime was on his head, and on his eyebrows, and his wiry chin. He carried his own low temperature always about with him; he iced his office in the dog-days, and didn't thaw it one degree at Christmas.

External heat and cold had little influence on Scrooge. No warmth could warm, nor wintry weather chill him. No wind that blew was bitterer than he, no falling snow was more intent upon its purpose, no pelting rain less open to entreaty. Foul weather didn't know where to have him. The heaviest rain, and snow, and hail and sleet, could boast of the advantage over him in only one respect. They often "came down" handsomely, and Scrooge never did.

CHARLES DICKENS, *A Christmas Carol.*


## 68.** THE VISITOR.

One midnight of a winter month the sleepers in Riversley Grange were awakened by a ringing of the outer bell and blows upon the great hall-doors....

It was a quiet grey night, and as the doors flew open, a

largely built man, dressed in a high-collared greatcoat and
fashionable hat of the time stood clearly defined to view. He
carried a light cane with the point of the silver handle against
his under lip. There was nothing formidable in his appearance,
and his manner was affectedly affable. He lifted his hat as
soon as he found himself face to face with the squire, disclosing
a partially bald head, though his whiskering was luxuriant,
and a robust condition of manhood was indicated by his erect
attitude and the immense swell of his furred greatcoat at the
chest. His features were exceedingly frank and cheerful. From
his superior height, he was enabled to look down quite royally
on the man whose repose he had disturbed.

GEORGE MEREDITH, *The Adventures of Harry Richmond.*

## 69.** THE ARCHDEACON.

As the archdeacon stood up to make his speech, erect in
the middle of that little square, he looked like an ecclesiastical
statue placed there, as a fitting impersonation of the church
militant here on earth; his shovel hat, large, new and well-
pronounced, a churchman's hat in every inch, declared the
profession as plainly as does the Quaker's broad brim; his
heavy eyebrow, large open eyes, and full mouth and chin
expressed the solidity of his order; the broad chest, amply
covered with fine cloth, told how well-to-do was its estate; one
hand, ensconced within his pocket, evinced the practical hold
which our mother church keeps on her temporal possessions,
and the other, loose for action, was ready to fight if need be
in her defence; and below these the decorous breeches, and
neat black gaiters showing so admirably that well-turned leg,
betokened the decency, the outward beauty, and grace of our
church establishment.        ANTHONY TROLLOPE, *The Warden.*

## 70.** MR BUNCE.

Immediately before him, on the extreme corner of the
bench which ran round the summer house, sat one old man,
with his handkerchief smoothly lain upon his knees. He was
one on whose large frame many years, for he was over eighty,

had made small havoc—he was still an upright, burly, handsome figure, with an open, ponderous brow, round which clung a few, though very few, thin grey locks. The coarse black gown of the hospital, the breeches, and buckled shoes became him well; and as he sat with his hands folded on his staff, and his chin resting on his hands, he was such a listener as most musicians would be glad to welcome. This man was certainly the pride of the hospital. It had always been the custom that one should be selected as being to some extent in authority over the others; and though Mr Bunce, for such was his name, and so he was always designated by his inferior brethren, had no greater emoluments than they, he had assumed, and well knew how to maintain, the dignity of his elevation.                 ANTHONY TROLLOPE, *The Warden.*

71.** AN ENGLISH STAGE-COACHMAN.

Wherever an English stage-coachman may be seen, he cannot be mistaken for any other craft or mystery.

He has commonly a broad, full face, curiously mottled with red, as if the blood had been forced by hard feeding into every vessel of the skin; he is swelled into jolly dimensions by frequent potations of malt liquors, and his bulk is still further increased by a multiplicity of coats, in which he is buried like a cauliflower, the upper one reaching to his heels. He wears a broad-brimmed, low-crowned hat; a huge roll of coloured handkerchief about his neck, knowingly knotted and tucked in at the bosom; and has in summertime a large bouquet of flowers in his buttonhole; the present, most probably, of some enamoured country lass. His waistcoat is commonly of some bright colour, striped, and his smallclothes extend far below the knees, to meet a pair of jockey-boots which reach about half-way up his legs.

All this costume is maintained with much precision; he has a pride in having his clothes of excellent materials; and, notwithstanding the seeming grossness of his appearance, there is still discernible that neatness and propriety of person which is almost inherent in an Englishman.

WASHINGTON IRVING, *The Sketch Book.*

### 72.** Mr Chester Coote.

There comes a gentlemanly figure into these events, and for a space takes a leading part therein, a Good Influence, a refined and amiable figure, Mr Chester Coote. You must figure him as about to enter our story, walking with a curious rectitude of bearing through the evening dusk towards the Public Library, erect, large-headed—he had a great big head, full of the suggestion of a powerful mind well under control—with a large official-looking envelope in his white and knuckly hand. In the other he carries a gold-handled cane. He wears a silken gray jacket suit, buttoned up, and anon he coughs behind the official envelope. He has a prominent nose, slaty gray eyes, and a certain heaviness about the mouth. His mouth hangs breathing open, with a slight protrusion of the lower jaw. His straw hat is pulled down a little in front, and he looks each person he passes in the eye, and, directly his look is answered, looks away.

Thus Mr Chester Coote, as he was on the evening when he came upon Kipps. He was a local house-agent, and a most active and gentlemanly person, a conscious gentleman, equally aware of society and the serious side of life. From amateur theatricals of a nice refined sort to science classes, few things were able to get along without him. He supplied a fine full bass, a little flat and quavery perhaps, but very abundant, to the St Stylites's choir....

He goes on towards the Public Library, lifts the envelope in salutation to a passing curate, smiles, and enters....

H. G. Wells, *Kipps.*

### III. NARRATIVE

### 73.* Giant Despair seizes Christian and Hopeful.

At last, lighting under a little shelter, they sat down there until the day brake; but, being weary, they fell asleep.

Now there was, not far from the place where they lay, a castle, called Doubting-castle, the owner whereof was Giant Despair, and it was in his grounds they now were sleeping;

wherefore he, getting up in the morning early, and walking up and down in his fields, caught Christian and Hopeful asleep in his grounds. Then with a grim and surly voice he bid them awake, and asked them whence they were, and what they did in his grounds. They told him they were pilgrims, and that they had lost their way. Then said the giant, "You have this night trespassed on me by trampling in and lying on my grounds, and therefore you must go along with me."

So they were forced to go, because he was stronger than they. They also had but little to say, for they knew themselves in a fault. The giant, therefore, drove them before him, and put them into his castle, into a very dark dungeon, nasty and stinking to the spirits of these two men.

JOHN BUNYAN, *The Pilgrim's Progress.*

### 74.** THE FOOT-PRINT IN THE SAND.

It happened one day, about noon, going towards my boat, I was exceedingly surprised with the print of a man's naked foot on the shore, which was very plain to be seen in the sand. I stood like one thunderstruck, or as if I had seen an apparition; I listened, I looked round me, but I could hear nothing, nor see anything; I went up to a rising ground to look further; but it was all one; I could see no other impression but that one.

I went to it again to see if there were any more, and to observe if it might not be my fancy; but there was no room for that, for there was exactly the very print of a foot, toes, heel, and every part of a foot: how it came thither I knew not, nor could in the least imagine; but, after innumerable fluttering thoughts, like a man perfectly confused and out of myself, I came home to my fortification, not feeling, as we say, the ground I went on, but terrified to the last degree; looking behind me at every two or three steps, mistaking every bush and tree, and fancying every stump at a distance to be a man.

DANIEL DEFOE, *Robinson Crusoe.*

### 75.* SAVED?

Well, all of a sudden, a coble, with a brown sail and a pair of fishers aboard of it, came flying round that corner of the isle, bound for Iona. I shouted out, and then fell on my knees on the rock and reached up my hands and prayed to them. They were near enough to hear—I could even see the colour of their hair—and there was no doubt but they observed me, for they cried out in the Gaelic tongue, and laughed. But the boat never turned aside, and flew on, right before my eyes, for Iona.

I could not believe such wickedness, and ran along the shore from rock to rock, crying on them piteously; even after they were out of reach of my voice, I still cried and waved to them; and when they were quite gone, I thought my heart would have burst.

R. L. STEVENSON, *Kidnapped.*

### 76.* SAVED? (*continued*).

The next day (which was the fourth of this horrible life of mine) I found my bodily strength run very low. But the sun shone, the air was sweet, and what I managed to eat of the shell-fish agreed well with me and revived my courage.

I was scarce back on my rock (where I went always the first thing after I had eaten) before I observed a boat coming down the Sound, and with her head, as I thought, in my direction.

I began at once to hope and fear exceedingly; for I thought these men might have thought better of their cruelty and be coming back to my assistance. But another disappointment, such as yesterday's, was more than I could bear. I turned my back, accordingly, upon the sea, and did not look again till I had counted many hundreds.

The boat was still heading for the island. The next time I counted the full thousand, as slowly as I could, my heart beating so as to hurt me. And then it was out of all question. She was coming straight to Earraid!

R. L. STEVENSON, *Kidnapped.*

## 77.** THE FLIGHT.

Sometimes we walked, sometimes ran; and as it drew on to morning, walked ever the less and ran the more. Though, upon its face, that country appeared to be a desert, yet there were huts and houses of the people, of which we must have passed more than twenty, hidden in quiet places of the hills. When we came to one of these, Alan would leave me in the way, and go himself and rap upon the side of the house and speak a little at the window with some speaker awakened.

This was to pass the news; which, in that country, was so much of a duty that Alan must pause to attend to it even while fleeing for his life; and so well attended to by others, that in more than half of the houses where we called they had heard already of the murder. In the others, as well as I could make out (standing back at a distance and hearing a strange tongue), the news was received with more of consternation than surprise.

R. L. STEVENSON, *Kidnapped*.

## 78.* THE CHILDREN'S WELCOME.

To-day I paid a visit to an old friend, who was formerly my schoolfellow. He came to town last week with his family for the winter, and yesterday morning sent me word his wife expected me to dinner. I am, as it were, at home at that house, and every member of it knows me intimately. I cannot indeed express the pleasure it is, to be met by the children with so much joy as I am, when I go there. The boys and girls strive who shall come first, when they think it is I who am knocking at the door.

To-day I was led in by a pretty girl, who we all thought must have forgotten me; for the family has been out of town these two years. Her knowing me again was a great pleasure to me and was the first subject of our conversation, after I entered. Then they began to tease me about a thousand little stories they had heard in the country, about my marriage to one of my neighbour's daughters. Upon which my friend said: "Nay, if Mr Bickerstaff marries a child of any of his old companions, I hope mine shall have the preference."

Sir RICHARD STEELE.

4—2

### 79.** SHY CAROL-SINGERS.

When I woke the next morning, it seemed as if all the events
of the preceding evening had been a dream, and nothing but
the identity of the ancient chamber convinced me of their
reality. While I lay musing on my pillow, I heard the sound
of little feet pattering outside of the door, and a whispering
consultation. Presently a choir of small voices chanted forth
an old Christmas carol, the burden of which was:

> Rejoice, our Saviour he was born
> On Christmas day in the morning.

I rose softly, slipped on my clothes, opened the door
suddenly, and beheld one of the most beautiful little fairy
groups that a painter could imagine. It consisted of a boy and
two girls, the eldest not morè than six, and lovely as seraphs.
They were going the rounds of the house, and singing at every
chamber door; but my sudden appearance frightened them
into mute bashfulness. They remained for a moment playing
on their lips with their fingers, and now and then stealing a shy
glance, from under their eyebrows, until, as if by one impulse,
they scampered away, and as they turned an angle of the
gallery, I heard them laughing in triumph at their escape.

WASHINGTON IRVING, *The Sketch Book.*

### 80.** THE BOYHOOD OF FIONN.

Fionn was brought to the wood of Slieve Bloom and was
nursed there in secret.

It is likely the women were fond of him, for other than
Fionn there was no life about them. He would be their life;
and their eyes may have seemed as twin benedictions resting
on the small fair head. He was fair-haired, and it was for his
fairness that he was afterwards known as Deimne. They saw
the food they put into his little frame reproduce itself length-
ways and sideways in tough inches, and in springs and energies
that crawled at first, and then toddled, and then ran. He had
birds for playmates, but all the creatures that live in a wood
must have been his comrades. There would have been for

little Fionn long hours of lonely sunshine, when the world seemed just sunshine and a sky. There would have been hours as long, when existence passed like a shade among shadows, in the multitudinous tappings of rain that dripped from leaf to leaf in the wood, and slipped so to the ground. He would have known little snaky paths, narrow enough to be filled by his own small feet, or a goat's; and he would have wondered where they went, and have marvelled again to find that, wherever they went, they came at last, through loops and twists of the branchy wood, to his own door. He may have thought of his own door as the beginning and end of the world, whence all things went, and whither all things came.

JAMES STEPHENS, *Irish Fairy Tales.*

### 81.* FIONN'S MOTHER COMES TO SEE HIM.

When he was six years of age his mother, beautiful, long-haired Muirne, came to see him. She came secretly, for she feared the sons of Morna, and she had paced through lonely places in many counties before she reached the hut in the wood, and the cot where he lay with his fists shut and sleep gripped in them.

He awakened to be sure. He would have one ear that would catch an unusual voice, one eye that would open, however sleepy the other one was. She took him in her arms and kissed him, and she sang a sleepy song until the small boy slept again.

We may be sure that the eye that could stay open stayed open that night as long as it could, and that the one ear listened to the sleepy song until the song got too low to be heard, until it was too tender to be felt vibrating along those soft arms, until Fionn was asleep again, with a new picture in his little head and a new notion to ponder on.

The mother of himself! His own mother!

But when he awakened she was gone.

She was going back secretly, in dread of the sons of Morna, slipping through gloomy woods, keeping away from habitations, getting by desolate and lonely ways to her lord in Kerry.

JAMES STEPHENS, *Irish Fairy Tales.*

## 82.* TACKLING THE SCHOOLMASTER.

It was a very small village. The men and boys were playing at cricket on the green, and as the other folks were looking on, they wandered up and down, uncertain where to seek a humble lodging. There was but one old man in the little garden before his cottage, and him they were timid of approaching, for he was the schoolmaster, and had "School" written up over his window in black letters on a white board. He was a pale, simple-looking man, of a spare and meagre habit, and sat among his flowers and beehives, smoking his pipe, in the little porch before his door.

"Speak to him, dear," the old man whispered.

"I am almost afraid to disturb him," said the child timidly.

"He does not seem to see us. Perhaps if we wait a little, he may look this way."

They waited, but the schoolmaster cast no look towards them, and still sat, thoughtful and silent, in the little porch....

As nobody else appeared and it would soon be dark, Nell at length took courage, and when he had resumed his pipe and seat, ventured to draw near, leading her grandfather by the hand.

CHARLES DICKENS, *The Old Curiosity Shop*.


## 83.** CROSSED IN LOVE.

In her short visits to some relations at Lausanne, the wit, the beauty, and erudition of Mademoiselle Curchod were the theme of universal applause. The report of such a prodigy awakened my curiosity; I saw and loved. I found her learned without pedantry, lively in conversation, pure in sentiment, and elegant in manners; and the first sudden emotion was fortified by the habits and knowledge of a more familiar acquaintance. She permitted me to make her two or three visits at her father's house. I passed some happy days there, in the mountains of Burgundy, and her parents honourably encouraged the connection. In a calm retirement the gay vanity of youth no longer fluttered in her bosom; she listened to the voice of truth and passion, and I might presume to hope that I had made some impression on a virtuous heart.

At Crassy and Lausanne I indulged my dream of felicity; but on my return to England, I soon discovered that my father would not hear of this strange alliance, and that without his consent I was myself destitute and helpless. After a painful struggle I yielded to my fate: I sighed as a lover, I obeyed as a son; my wound was insensibly healed by time, absence, and the habits of a new life. My cure was accelerated by a faithful report of the tranquillity and cheerfulness of the lady herself, and my love subsided in friendship and esteem....Mademoiselle Curchod is now the wife of M. Necker, the minister, and perhaps the legislator, of the French monarchy.

EDWARD GIBBON, *Memoirs of my Life and Writings.*

## 84.* A DISABLED SOLDIER'S STORY.

I was born in Shropshire, my father was a labourer, and died when I was five years old; so I was put upon the parish. As he had been a wandering sort of a man, the parishioners were not able to tell to what parish I belonged, or where I was born, so they sent me to another parish, and that parish sent me to a third. I thought in my heart, they kept sending me about so long that they would not let me be born in any parish at all; but, at last, however, they fixed me. I had some disposition to be a scholar, and was resolved, at least, to know my letters; but the master of the work-house put me to business as soon as I was able to handle a mallet; and here I lived an easy kind of life for five years. I only wrought ten hours in the day, and had my meat and drink provided by my labour. It is true, I was not suffered to stir out of the house, for fear, as they said, I should run away; but what of that, I had the liberty of the whole house, and the yard before the door, and that was enough for me. I was then bound out to a farmer, where I was up both early and late; but I ate and drank well, and liked my business well enough, till he died, when I was obliged to provide for myself; so I was resolved to go seek my fortune.

OLIVER GOLDSMITH.

## 85.* THE CAPTAIN'S TALE.

"As I was once sailing," said he, "in a fine stout ship across the banks of Newfoundland, one of those heavy fogs which prevail in those parts rendered it impossible for us to see far ahead, even in the day-time; but at night the weather was so thick that we could not distinguish any object at twice the length of the ship. I kept lights at the mast-head, and a constant watch forward to look out for fishing smacks, which are accustomed to lie at anchor on the banks. The wind was blowing a smacking breeze, and we were going at a great rate through the water.

"Suddenly the watch gave the alarm of 'a sail ahead!'—it was scarcely uttered before we were upon her. She was a small schooner, at anchor, with her broadside towards us. The crew were all asleep, and had neglected to hoist a light. We struck her just amid-ships. The force, the size, and weight of our vessel bore her down below the waves; we passed over her, and were hurried on our course. As the crashing wreck was sinking beneath us, I had a glimpse of two or three half-naked wretches rushing from her cabin: they just started from their beds to be swallowed shrieking by the waves. I heard their drowning cry mingling with the wind. The blast that bore it to our ears swept us out of all further hearing. I shall never forget that cry!

"It was some time before we could put the ship about, she was under such head-way. We returned, as nearly as we could guess, to the place where the smack had anchored...but all was silent—we never saw or heard anything of them more."

WASHINGTON IRVING, *The Sketch Book.*

## 86.** MAN OVERBOARD!

I was on the forecastle, discoursing with two of the sailors: one of them, who had just left his hammock, said, "I have had a strange dream, which I do not much like; for," continued he, pointing up to the mast, "I dreamt that I fell into the sea from the cross-trees." He was heard to say this by several of the crew besides myself.

A moment later, the captain of the vessel perceiving that the squall was increasing, ordered the top-sails to be taken in; whereupon this man, with several others, instantly ran aloft. The yard was in the act of being hauled down, when a sudden gust of wind whirled it round with violence, and a man was struck down from the cross-trees into the sea, which was working like yeast below. In a few moments he emerged. I saw his head on the crest of a billow, and instantly recognized in the unfortunate man the sailor who, a few moments before, had related his dream. I shall never forget the look of agony he cast whilst the steamer hurried past him.

The alarm was given, and everything was in confusion. It was two minutes at least before the vessel was stopped, by which time the man was a considerable way astern. I still, however, kept my eye upon him, and could see that he was struggling gallantly with the waves. A boat was at length lowered; but the rudder was unfortunately not at hand, and only two oars could be procured, with which the men could make but little progress in so rough a sea. They did their best, however, and had arrived within ten yards of the man, who still struggled for his life, when I lost sight of him; and the men on their return said that they saw him below the water, at glimpses, sinking deeper and deeper, his arms stretched out and his body apparently stiff, but that they found it impossible to save him. Presently after, the sea, as if satisfied with the prey which it had acquired, became comparatively calm.

GEORGE BORROW, *The Bible in Spain.*

### 87.** WHY SHIPS ARE POSTED "MISSING."

Wallowing as if she meant to turn over with us, the barque, her decks full of water, her gear flying in bights, ran at some ten knots an hour. We had been driven far south—much farther that way than we had meant to go; and suddenly, up there in the slings of the foreyard, in the midst of our work, I felt my shoulder gripped with such force in the carpenter's powerful paw that I positively yelled with unexpected pain. The man's eyes stared close in my face, and he shouted, "Look, sir! look! What's this?" pointing ahead with his other hand.

At first I saw nothing. The sea was one empty wilderness of black and white hills. Suddenly, half-concealed in the tumult of the foaming rollers I made out awash, something enormous, rising and falling—something spread out like a burst of foam, but with a more bluish, more solid look.

It was a piece of an ice-floe melted down to a fragment, but still big enough to sink a ship, and floating lower than any raft, right in our way, as if ambushed among the waves with murderous intent. There was no time to get down on deck. I shouted from aloft till my head was ready to split. I was heard aft, and we managed to clear the sunken floe which had come all the way from the Southern ice-cap to have a try at our unsuspecting lives. Had it been an hour later, nothing could have saved the ship, for no eye could have made out in the dusk that pale piece of ice swept over by the white-crested waves.

JOSEPH CONRAD, *The Mirror of the Sea.*

### 88.* NELSON'S FAREWELL.

Then, in a stronger voice, he said, "Anchor, Hardy, anchor." Hardy upon this hinted that Admiral Collingwood would take upon himself the direction of affairs. "Not while I live, Hardy!" said the dying Nelson, ineffectually endeavouring to raise himself from the bed. "Do you anchor." His previous order for preparing to anchor had shown how clearly he foresaw the necessity of this.

Presently, calling Hardy back, he said to him, in a low voice, "Don't throw me overboard"; and he desired that he might be buried by his parents, unless it should please the king to order otherwise. Then, reverting to private feelings, "Take care of my dear Lady Hamilton, Hardy: take care of poor Lady Hamilton."—"Kiss me, Hardy," said he. Hardy knelt down and kissed his cheek: and Nelson said, "Now I am satisfied. Thank God I have done my duty."

Hardy stood over him in silence for a moment or two, then knelt again, and kissed his forehead. "Who is that?" said Nelson; and being informed, he replied, "God bless you Hardy." And Hardy then left him—for ever.

ROBERT SOUTHEY, *Life of Nelson.*

### 89.* THE DEATH OF SHELLEY.

I trust that the first news of the dreadful calamity which has befallen us here will have been broken to you by report, otherwise I shall come on you with a most painful abruptness; but Shelley, my divine-minded friend, your friend, the friend of the universe, he has perished at sea.

He was going in a boat with his friend Captain Williams, going from Leghorn to Lerici, when a storm arose, and it is supposed the boat must have foundered. It was on the 8th instant, about four or five in the evening, they guess. A fisherman says he saw the boat a few minutes before it went down; he looked again and it was gone. He saw the boy they had with them aloft furling one of the sails.

We hope his story is true, as their passage from life to death will then have been short; and what adds to the hope is, that in S.'s pocket (for the bodies were both thrown on shore some days afterwards,—conceive our horrible certainty, after trying all we could to hope!) a copy of Keats's last volume, which he had borrowed of me to read on his passage, was found *open* and doubled back as if it had been thrust in, in the hurry of a surprise.

I cannot help thinking of him as if he were alive as much as ever, so unearthly he always appeared to me, and so seraphical a thing of the elements; and this is what all his friends say.

LEIGH HUNT, *Letter to Horace Smith*, Pisa, 25 July, 1822.

### 90.* THE KING LAY DYING.

It was not very quiet in the room where the king lay dying. People were coming and going, rustling in and out with hushed footsteps, whispering eagerly to each other; and where a great many people are all busy making as little noise as possible, the result is apt to be a kind of bustle, that weakened nerves can scarcely endure.

But what did that matter? The doctors said he could hear nothing now. He gave no sign that he could. Surely the sobs of his beautiful young wife, as she knelt by the bedside, must else have moved him.

For days the light had been carefully shaded. Now, in the hurry, confusion and distress, no one remembered to draw the curtains close, so that the dim eyes might not be dazzled. But what did that matter? The doctors said that he could see nothing now.

For days no one but his attendants had been allowed to come near him. Now the room was free for all who chose to enter. What did it matter? The doctors said he knew no one.

MARY COLERIDGE, *The King is dead, Long live the King.*

### 91.* IN THEIR DEATH THEY WERE NOT DIVIDED.

"Park House stands high up out of the flood," said Maggie, "perhaps they have got Lucy there."

Nothing else was said; a new danger was being carried towards them by the river. Some wooden machinery had just given way on one of the wharves, and huge fragments were being floated along. The sun was rising now, and the wide area of watery desolation was spread out in dreadful clearness around them—in dreadful clearness floated onwards the hurrying, threatening masses. A large company in a boat that was working its way along under the Tofton houses, observed their danger, and shouted, "Get out of the current!"

But that could not be done at once, and Tom, looking before him, saw death rushing on them. Huge fragments, clinging together in fatal fellowship, made one wide mass across the stream.

"It is coming, Maggie;" Tom said, in a deep hoarse voice, loosing the oars, and clasping her.

The next instant the boat was no longer seen upon the water—and the huge mass was hurrying on in hideous triumph.

But soon the keel of the boat reappeared, a black speck on the golden water.

The boat reappeared—but brother and sister had gone down in an embrace never to be parted: living through again in one supreme moment the days when they had clasped their little hands in love, and roamed the daisied fields together.

GEORGE ELIOT, *The Mill on the Floss.*

## 92.** A Dramatic Incident.

"Noble Crawford," said Orleans, who had now entirely re-
covered from his swoon, "you are too like in character to your
friend Dunois, not to do him justice. It was indeed I that
dragged him hither, most unwillingly, upon an enterprise of
harebrained passion, suddenly and rashly undertaken. Look
on me all who will," he added, rising up and turning to the
soldiery, "I am Louis of Orleans, willing to pay the penalty of
my own folly. I trust the King will limit his displeasure to
me, as is but just. Meanwhile, as a Child of France must not
give up his sword to any one—not even to you, brave Crawford
—fare-thee-well, good steel."

So saying, he drew his sword from its scabbard and flung
it into the lake. It went through the air like a stream of lightning, and sunk in the flashing waters, which speedily closed
over it. All remained standing in irresolution and astonishment, so high was the rank and so much esteemed was the
character of the culprit; while, at the same time, all were conscious that the consequences of his rash enterprise, considering
the views which the King had upon him, were likely to end in
his utter ruin.

Sir WALTER SCOTT, *Quentin Durward.*


## 93.* Redgauntlet's Farewell.

"And now I shall not need that pardon," said Redgauntlet.
"I leave England for ever; but I am not displeased that you
should hear my family adieus. Nephew, come thither. In
presence of General Campbell I tell you that, though to breed
you up in my own political opinions has been for many years
my anxious wish, I am now glad that it could not be accomplished. You pass under the service of the reigning Monarch
without the necessity of changing your allegiance—a change,
however," he added, looking around him, "which sits more
easy on honourable men than I could have anticipated; but
some wear the badge of their loyalty on their sleeve, and
others in the heart. You will from henceforth be uncontrolled

master of all the property of which forfeiture could not de-
prive your father—of all that belonged to him—excepting
this, his good sword" (laying his hand on the weapon he wore),
"which shall never fight for the House of Hanover; and as
my hand will never draw weapon more, I shall sink it forty
fathoms deep in the wide ocean. Bless you, young man! If I
have dealt harshly with you, forgive me. I had set my whole
desires on one point—God knows, with no selfish purpose;
and I am justly punished by this final termination of my
views, for having been too little scrupulous in the means by
which I pursued them. Niece, farewell, and may God bless
you also!"          Sir WALTER SCOTT, *Redgauntlet.*

### 94.* JOHNSON AND GOLDSMITH.

"I received one morning," Johnson told me, "a message
from poor Goldsmith that he was in great distress, and, as it
was not in his power to come to me, begging that I would
come to him as soon as possible. I sent him a guinea, and
promised to come to him directly. I according went as soon
as I was drest, and found that his landlady had arrested him
for his rent, at which he was in a violent passion. I perceived
that he had already changed my guinea and had got a bottle
of Madeira and a glass before him. I put the cork into the
bottle, desired he would be calm, and began to talk to him of
the means by which he might be extricated. He then told
me he had a novel ready for the press, which he produced to
me. I looked into it, and saw its merit; told the landlady I
should soon return, and, having gone to a bookseller, sold it
for sixty pounds. I brought Goldsmith the money, and he
discharged his rent, not without rating his landlady in a high
tone for having used him so ill."

JAMES BOSWELL, *Life of Samuel Johnson.*

### 95.* POOR PETER.

Then my mother told me what had happened, and that she
was going up to Peter's room, at my father's desire—though
she was not to tell Peter this—to talk the matter over with

him. But no Peter was there. We looked over the house;
no Peter was there! Even my father, who had not liked to
join in the search at first, helped us before long. The Rectory
was a very old house: steps up into a room, steps down into a
room, all through. At first my mother went calling low and soft
—as if to reassure the poor boy—"Peter! Peter dear! its only
me"; but, by and by, as the servants came back from the errands
my father had sent them, in different directions, to find where
Peter was—as we found he was not in the garden, nor the
hayloft, nor anywhere about—my mother's cry grew louder
and wilder—"Peter! Peter, my darling! where are you?" for
then she felt and understood that that long kiss meant some
sad kind of "good-bye."         Mrs GASKELL, *Cranford*.

### 96.* POOR PETER (*continued*).

The afternoon went on—my mother never resting, but seeking again and again in every possible place that had been looked
into twenty times before; nay, that she had looked into over
and over again herself. My father sat with his head in his
hands, not speaking, except when his messengers came in,
bringing no tidings; then he lifted up his face so strong and
sad, and told them to go again in some new direction. My
mother kept passing from room to room, in and out of the
house, moving noiselessly, but never ceasing. Neither she nor
my father durst leave the house, which was the meeting-place
for all the messengers.

At last (and it was nearly dark), my father rose up. He
took hold of my mother's arm, as she came with wild, sad
pace, through one door, and quickly towards another. She
started at the touch of his hand, for she had forgotten all in
the world but Peter.         Mrs GASKELL, *Cranford*.

### 97.* THE HEROIC BUTLER.

When Lady Glenmire came, we almost felt jealous of her.
Mrs Jamieson's house had really been attacked; at least there
were men's footsteps to be seen on the flower-borders, underneath the kitchen windows "where nae men should be"; and

Carlo had barked all through the night as if strangers were abroad. Mrs Jamieson had been awakened by Lady Glenmire, and they had rung the bell which communicated with Mr Mulliner's room, in the third story, and when his night-capped head had appeared over the bannisters, in answer to the summons, they had told him of their alarm, and the reasons for it; whereupon he retreated into his bedroom and locked the door (for fear of draughts, as he informed them in the morning), and opened the window, and called out valiantly to say, if the supposed robbers would come to him he would fight them; but, as Lady Glenmire observed, that was but poor comfort, since they would have to pass by Mrs Jamieson's room and her own, before they could reach him, and must be of a very pugnacious disposition indeed, if they neglected the opportunities of robbery presented by the unguarded lower stories to go up to a garret, and there force a door in order to get at the champion of the house.

Lady Glenmire, after waiting and listening for some time in the drawing-room, had proposed to Mrs Jamieson that they should go to bed; but that lady said she should not feel comfortable unless she sat up and watched; and, accordingly, she packed herself warmly up on the sofa, where she was found by the housemaid, when she came into the room at six o'clock, fast asleep; but Lady Glenmire went to bed, and kept awake all night.                    Mrs GASKELL, *Cranford*.

### 98.** THE STORY OF A GOLD-HEADED CANE.

I remember reading a story of an old gentleman who used to walk out every afternoon, with a gold-headed cane, in the fields opposite Baltimore House. He was frequently accosted by a beggar with a wooden leg, to whom he gave money, which only made him more importunate. One day, when he was more troublesome than usual, a well-dressed person happening to come up, and observing how saucy the fellow was, said to the gentleman, "Sir, if you will lend me your cane for a moment, I'll give him a good thrashing for his impertinence."

The old gentleman, smiling at the proposal, handed him his

cane, which the other no sooner was going to apply to the shoulders of the culprit, than he immediately whipped off his wooden leg, and scampered off with great alacrity, and his chastiser after him as hard as he could go. The faster the one ran, the faster the other followed him, brandishing the cane, to the great astonishment of the gentleman who owned it, till, having fairly crossed the fields, they suddenly turned a corner, and nothing more was seen of either of them.

WILLIAM HAZLITT, *Wit and Humour.*

### 99.* THE EAGLE'S LAST SWOOP.

Like all true sportsmen, Struan Robertson was a naturalist,— studied Nature's ongoings and all her children with a keen, unerring and loving eye, from her lichens and moths (for which Rannoch is famous) to her eagles, red deer and *Salmo ferox*; and his stories, if recorded, would stand well side by side with Mr St John's. One we remember. He and his keeper were on a cloudless day in mid-winter walking across the head of Loch Rannoch, which, being shallow, was frozen over. The keeper stopped, and, looking straight up into the clear sky, said to his master, "Do you see that?" Keen as he was, Struan said, "What?" "An eagle"; and there, sure enough, was a mere speck in the far-off "azure depths of air." Duncan Roy flung a white hare he had shot along the ice, and instantly the speck darkened, and down came the mighty creature with a swoop, and not knowing of the ice, was "made a round flat dish of, with the head in the centre."    Dr JOHN BROWN.

### 100.*** HOW BECKY SHARP RECEIVED HER SITUATION.

Worthy Miss Pinkerton, although she had a Roman nose and a turban, and was as tall as a grenadier, and had been up to this time an irresistible princess, had no will or strength like that of her little apprentice, and in vain did battle against her, and tried to overawe her. Attempting once to scold her in public, Rebecca hit upon the before-mentioned plan of answering her in French, which quite routed the old woman.

In order to maintain authority in her school, it became necessary to remove this rebel, this monster, this serpent, this firebrand; and hearing about this time that Sir Pitt Crawley's family was in want of a governess, she actually recommended Miss Sharp for the situation, firebrand and serpent as she was. "I cannot, certainly," she said, "find fault with Miss Sharp's conduct, except to myself; and must allow that her talents and accomplishments are of a high order. As far as the head goes, at least, she does credit to the educational system pursued at my establishment."

W. M. THACKERAY, Vanity Fair.

101.*** A STAGE ENTRY.

Assuredly, by far the most tremendous stage entries I ever saw were those of Mr Wilson Barrett in his later days, the days when he had become his own dramatist. I remember particularly a first night of his at which I happened to be sitting next to a clever but not very successful and rather sardonic old actor. I forget just what great historic or mythic personage Mr Barrett was to represent, but I know that the earlier scenes of the play resounded with rumours of him—accounts of the great deeds he had done, and of the yet greater deeds that were expected of him. And at length there was a procession: white-bearded priests bearing wands; maidens playing upon the sackbut; guards in full armour; a pell-mell of unofficial citizens ever prancing along the edge of the pageant, huzza-ing and hosanna-ing, mostly looking back over their shoulders and shading their eyes; maidens strewing rose-leaves; and at last the orchestra crashing to a climax in the nick of which my neighbour turned to me and, with an assumption of innocent enthusiasm, whispered, "I shouldn't *wonder* if this were Barrett." I suppose (Mr Barrett at that instant amply appearing) I gave way to laughter; but this didn't matter; the applause would have drowned a thunderstorm, and lasted for several minutes.

MAX BEERBOHM, And Even Now.

## 102.* A Station Incident.

Some years ago I arrived at the Gare St Lazare at Paris two or three days before the August Bank Holiday about half an hour before the time of my train. I had sent my luggage an hour in advance, but when I got to the station it was still in the courtyard. There was a long queue of people waiting to have their luggage weighed and registered and I saw that I had no chance of catching the train at the rate at which things were moving. I went into the luggage-hall and saw that of four weighing-machines only one was being used, which accounted for the delay. I protested so vigorously that the station-master was sent for and immediately ordered all the four machines to be put in use. The other passengers were so grateful to me that they insisted on my luggage being weighed first, quite out of my turn. The strange thing was that, although some of them had been there for a couple of hours, not one had thought of doing what I did; but for my English impatience, three-fourths of them would have missed their trains, and then there would probably have been a small riot.

Now this incident is typical of the French attitude towards authority; the French will too often endure abuses for years without making any effective protest, and when at last the situation becomes absolutely unbearable they will break out and smash up everything. That is the reason why there have been so many revolutions in France; nobody thinks of making reforms until it is too late and a clean sweep has become inevitable.

ROBERT DELL, *My Second Country (France).*

## IV. HISTORICAL

### 103.** THE CHURCH OF ROME.

There is not, and there never was on this earth, a work of human policy so well deserving of examination as the Roman Catholic Church. The history of that Church joins together the two great ages of human civilization. No other institution is left standing which carries the mind back to the times when the smoke of sacrifice rose from the Pantheon, and when camelopards and tigers bounded in the Flavian amphitheatre. The proudest royal houses are but of yesterday, when compared with the line of the Supreme Pontiffs.

That line we trace back in an unbroken series, from the Pope who crowned Napoleon in the nineteenth century to the Pope who crowned Pepin in the eighth; and far beyond the time of Pepin the august dynasty extends, till it is lost in the twilight of fable. The republic of Venice came next in antiquity. But the republic of Venice was modern when compared with the Papacy; and the republic of Venice is gone, and the Papacy remains.

Lord MACAULAY, *Essays.*

### 104.** THE CHURCH OF ROME (*continued*).

The Papacy remains, not in decay, not a mere antique, but full of life and youthful vigour. The Catholic Church is still sending forth to the farthest ends of the world missionaries as zealous as those who landed in Kent with Augustin, and still confronting hostile kings with the same spirit with which she confronted Attila. The number of her children is greater than in any former age....

Nor do we see any sign which indicates that the term of her long dominion is approaching. She saw the commencement of all the governments and of all the ecclesiastical establishments that now exist in the world; and we feel no assurance that she is not destined to see the end of them all. She was great and respected before the Saxon had set foot on Britain, before the Frank had passed the Rhine, when Grecian eloquence still flourished in Antioch, when idols were still worshipped in the temple of Mecca. And she may still exist in undiminished vigour when some traveller from New Zealand shall, in the midst of a vast solitude, take his stand on a broken arch of London Bridge to sketch the ruins of St Paul's.

Lord MACAULAY, *Essays.*

### 105.* THE ORIGINS OF MODERN ENGLAND.

In no country has the enmity of race been carried farther than in England. In no country has that enmity been more completed effaced. When John became King, the distinction between Saxons and Normans was strongly marked, but before the end of the reign of his grandson it had almost disappeared. In the time of Richard the First, the ordinary imprecation of a Norman gentleman was "May I become an Englishman!" His ordinary form of indignant denial was "Do you take me for an Englishman?" The descendant of such a gentleman a hundred years later was proud of the English name.

The sources of the noblest rivers which spread fertility over continents, and bear richly laden fleets to the sea, are to be sought in wild and barren mountain tracts, incorrectly laid down in maps, and rarely explored by travellers. To such a tract the history of our country during the thirteenth century may not inaptly be compared. Sterile and obscure as is that portion of our annals, it is there that we must seek for the origin of our freedom, our prosperity, and our glory.

Lord MACAULAY, *History of England.*

### 106.** THE RETURN OF COLUMBUS.

To receive him with suitable pomp and distinction, the sovereigns had ordered their throne to be placed in public, under a rich canopy of brocade of gold, in a vast and splendid saloon. Here the king and queen awaited his arrival, seated in state, with the prince Juan beside them; and attended by the dignitaries of their Court and the principal nobility of Castile, Valencia, Catalonia, and Arragon; all impatient to behold the man who had conferred so incalculable a benefit upon the nation. At length Columbus entered the hall, surrounded by a brilliant crowd of cavaliers, among whom, says Las Casas, he was conspicuous for his stately and commanding person, which, with his countenance rendered venerable by his grey hairs, gave him the august appearance of a senator of Rome.

A modest smile lighted up his features, showing that he enjoyed the state and glory in which he came; and certainly nothing could be more deeply moving to a mind inflamed by noble ambition, and conscious of having greatly deserved, than these testimonials of the admiration and gratitude of a nation, or rather of a world. As Columbus approached, the sovereigns rose, as if receiving a person of the highest rank. Bending his knees, he requested to kiss their hands; but there was some hesitation on the part of their majesties to permit this act of vassalage. Raising him in the most gracious manner, they ordered him to seat himself in their presence; a rare honour in this proud and punctilious Court.

WASHINGTON IRVING.

## 107.** THE COLONIZATION OF AMERICA.

What a contrast did these children of Southern Europe present to the Anglo-Saxon races, who scattered themselves along the great northern division of the western hemisphere! For the principle of action with these latter was not avarice, nor the more specious pretext of proselytism, but independence—independence religious and political. To secure this, they were content to earn a bare subsistence by a life of frugality and toil. They asked nothing from the soil but the reasonable returns of their own labour. No golden visions threw a deceitful halo around their path, and beckoned them onwards through seas of blood to the subversion of an unoffending dynasty.

They were content with the slow but steady progress of their social polity. They patiently endured the privations of the wilderness, watering the tree of liberty with their tears and with the sweat of their brow, till it took deep root in the land and sent up its branches high towards the heavens, while the communities of the neighbouring continent, shooting up into the sudden splendours of a tropical vegetation, exhibited, even in their prime, the sure symptoms of decay.

It would seem to have been especially ordered by Providence, that the discovery of the two great divisions of the American hemisphere should fall to the two races best fitted to conquer and colonize them. Thus the northern section was consigned to the Anglo-Saxon race, whose orderly industrious habits found an ample field for development under its colder skies and on its more rugged soil; while the southern portion, with its rich tropical products and treasures of mineral wealth, held out the most attractive bait to invite the enterprise of the Spaniard. How different might have been the result, if the bark of Columbus had taken a more northerly direction, as he at one time meditated, and landed its band of adventurers on the shores of what is now Protestant America!

W. H. PRESCOTT, *Conquest of Mexico.*

### 108.** SOLDIERS OF THE CROSS.

There was nothing which the Spanish Government had more earnestly at heart than the conversion of the Indians. It forms the constant burden of their instructions, and gave to the military expeditions in this Western Hemisphere somewhat of the air of a crusade. The cavalier who embarked in them entered fully into these chivalrous and devotional feelings. No doubt was entertained of the efficacy of conversion, however sudden might be the change, or however violent the means. The sword was a good argument when the tongue failed; and the spread of Mahometanism has shown that seeds sown by the hand of violence, far from perishing in the ground, would spring up and bear fruit to after time. If this were so in a bad cause, how much more would it be true in a good one! The Spanish cavalier felt he had a high mission to accomplish as a soldier of the Cross. However unauthorised or unrighteous the war into which he had entered may seem to us, to him it was a holy war. He was in arms against the infidel.

W. H. PRESCOTT, *Conquest of Mexico.*

### 109.** THE BIRTH OF THE MODERN WORLD.

For, indeed, a change was coming upon the world, the meaning and direction of which even still is hidden from us, a change from era to era. The paths trodden by the footsteps of ages were broken up; old things were passing away, and the faith and the life of ten centuries were dissolving like a dream. Chivalry was dying; the abbey and the castle were soon together to crumble into ruins; and all the forms, desires, beliefs, convictions of the old world were passing away never to return. A new continent had risen up beyond the western sea. The floor of heaven, inlaid with stars, had sunk back to an infinite abyss of immeasurable space; and the firm earth itself, unfixed from its foundations, was seen to be but a small atom in the awful vastness of the universe. In the fabric of habit which they had so laboriously built for themselves, mankind were to remain no longer.

And now it is all gone—like an unsubstantial pageant faded; and between us and the old English there lies a gulf of mystery which the prose of the historian will never adequately bridge. They cannot come to us, and our imagination can but feebly penetrate to them. Only among the aisles of the cathedral, only as we gaze upon their silent figures sleeping on their tombs, some faint conceptions float before us of what these men were when they were alive; and perhaps in the sound of church bells, that peculiar creation of mediæval age, which falls upon the ear like the echo of a vanished world.

J. A. FROUDE, *History of England.*

### 110.* CLIVE AT PLASSEY.

Clive was in a painfully anxious situation. He could place no confidence in the sincerity or in the courage of his confederate; and, whatever confidence he might place in his own military talents, and in the valour and discipline of his troops, it was no light thing to engage an army twenty times as numerous as his own. Before him lay a river over which it was easy to advance, but over which, if things went ill, not one of his little band would ever return.

On this occasion, for the first and for the last time, his dauntless spirit, during a few hours, shrank from the fearful responsibility of making a decision. He called a council of war. The majority pronounced against fighting; and Clive declared his concurrence with the majority. Long afterwards, he said that he had never called but one council of war, and that, if he had taken the advice of that council, the British would never have been masters of Bengal. But scarcely had the meeting broken up when he was himself again. He retired alone under the shade of some trees, and passed near an hour there in thought. He came back determined to put everything to the hazard, and gave orders that all should be in readiness for passing the river on the morrow.

Lord MACAULAY, Essays.

### III.** THE EXECUTION OF MARIE-ANTOINETTE.

At eleven, Marie-Antoinette was brought out. She had on an undress of *piqué blanc*: she was led to the place of execution, in the same manner as an ordinary criminal; bound, on a cart; accompanied by a Constitutional Priest in Lay dress; escorted by numerous detachments of infantry and cavalry. These, and the double row of troops all along her road, she appeared to regard with indifference. On her countenance there was visible neither abashment nor pride. To the cries of *Vive la République* and *Down with Tyranny*, which attended her all the way, she seemed to pay no heed. She spoke little to her Confessor. The tricolour Streamers on the housetops occupied her attention, in the Streets du Roule and Saint-Honoré; she also noticed the Inscriptions on the house-fronts. On reaching the Place de la Révolution, her looks turned towards the *Jardin National,* whilom Tuileries; her face at that moment gave signs of lively emotion. She mounted the Scaffold with courage enough; at a quarter past Twelve, her head fell; the Executioner showed it to the people, amid universal long-continued cries of *Vive la République.*

THOMAS CARLYLE, History of the French Revolution.

## 112.*** MARIE-ANTOINETTE.

It is now sixteen or seventeen years since I saw the Queen of France, then the Dauphiness, at Versailles; and surely never lighted on this orb, which she hardly seemed to touch, a more delightful vision. I saw her just above the horizon, decorating and cheering the elevated sphere she just began to move in; glittering like the morning star, full of life, and splendour, and joy. Oh! what a revolution! and what a heart must I have to contemplate without emotion that elevation and that fall! Little did I dream when she added titles of veneration to those of enthusiastic, distant, respectful love, that she should ever be obliged to carry the sharp antidote against disgrace concealed in that bosom; little did I dream that I should have lived to see such disasters fallen upon her in a nation of gallant men, in a nation of men of honour and of cavaliers. I thought ten thousand swords must have leaped from their scabbards to avenge even a look that threatened her with insult.

But the age of chivalry is gone. That of sophisters, economists, and calculators, has succeeded; and the glory of Europe is extinguished for ever. Never, never more, shall we behold that generous loyalty to rank and sex, that proud submission, that dignified obedience, that subordination of the heart, which kept alive, even in servitude itself, the spirit of an exalted freedom. The unbought grace of life, the cheap defence of nations, the nurse of manly sentiments and heroic enterprise is gone! It is gone that sensibility of principle, that chastity of honour, which felt a stain like a wound, which inspired courage whilst it mitigated ferocity, which ennobled whatever it touched, and under which vice itself lost half its evil, by losing all its grossness.

EDMUND BURKE, *Reflections on the Revolution in France.*

## 113.*** THE AGONIES OF A NATION.

It was well to pity the unmerited agonies of Marie-Antoinette, though as yet, we must remember, she had suffered nothing beyond the indignities of the days of October at Versailles. But did not the protracted agonies of a nation deserve the tribute of a tear? As Paine asked, were men to weep over the plumage, and forget the dying bird? The bulk of the people must labour, Burke told them, "to obtain what by labour can be obtained; and when they find, as they commonly do, the success disproportioned to the endeavour, they must be taught their consolation is the final proportion of eternal justice."

When we learn that a Lyons silk weaver, working as hard as he could for over seventeen hours a day, could not earn money enough to procure the most bare and urgent necessaries of subsistence, we may know with what benignity of brow eternal justice must have presented herself in the garret of that hapless wretch. It was no idle abstraction, no metaphysical right of man for which the French cried, but only the practical right of being permitted, by their own toil, to save themselves and the little ones about their knees from hunger and cruel death.

Viscount MORLEY, *Burke.*

### 114.*** THE ROMANCE OF EDINBURGH.

Down in the palace John Knox reproved his queen in the accents of modern democracy. In the town, in one of those little shops plastered like so many swallows' nests among the buttresses of the old Cathedral, that familiar autocrat, James VI, would gladly share a bottle of wine with George Heriot the goldsmith. Up on the Pentland Hills, that so quietly look down on the Castle with the city lying in waves around it, those mad and dismal fanatics, the Sweet Singers, haggard from long exposure on the moors, sat day and night with "tearful psalms" to see Edinburgh consumed with fire from heaven, like another Sodom or Gomorrah. There, in the Grass-Market, stiff-necked, covenanting heroes offered up the often unnecessary, but not less honourable, sacrifice of their lives, and bade eloquent farewell to sun, moon, and stars, and earthly friendships, or died silent to the roll of drums. Down by yon outlet rode Grahame of Claverhouse and his thirty dragoons, with the town beating to arms behind their horses' tails—a sorry handful thus riding for their lives, but with a man at the head who was to return in a different temper, make a dash that staggered Scotland to the heart, and die happily in the thick of fight. There Aikenhead was hanged for a piece of boyish incredulity; there, a few years afterwards, David Hume ruined Philosophy and Faith, an undisturbed and well-reputed citizen; and thither, in yet a few years more, Burns came from the plough-tail to an academy of gilt unbelief and artificial letters.

R. L. STEVENSON, Edinburgh.

### 115.** THE TRAGIC STORY.

There were bowmen of Poitiers who lived to hear of their sons wielding the firelock at Agincourt, when already Joan of Arc was listening at Domrémy to legends of English aggression. After she had fulfilled her destiny in withstanding the power of England, rarely a decade passed without renewal of Anglo-French hostilities, till the comparative peace maintained by the first Tudor Monarchs. Yet even in that amicable period there were three English invasions of France in half a century. Then followed the loss of Calais, Elizabeth's armed interventions on behalf of the Huguenots, and the expedition to La Rochelle, all within seventy years. When England ceased to be ruled by a king, and France was governed by a foreign priest, Cromwell and Mazarin agreed to keep the peace for a short season; but all the love of Charles II for Louis XIV could not prevent their two nations coming to blows, and in 1666 we were actually at war with France. The military inaction forced on the English by the last of the Stuart line ceased, after the flight of James II, with the French invasion of Ireland, followed forthwith by the sea-fight of La Hogue. Then Blenheim was only a dozen years distant, and there were young soldiers of Marlborough and of Villars at Malplaquet who fought as veterans at Fontenoy. Only seventy years then remained to Waterloo, a blood-stained period as crowded with French and British encounters as that of the Hundred Years' War with which this recapitulation began.

J. E. C. BODLEY, France.

## 116.* THE CHARGE OF THE OLD GUARD.

At half-past four the advance guard of the Prussians deployed at last from the woods; but the main body was far behind, and Napoleon was still able to hold his ground against them till their increasing masses forced him to stake all on a desperate effort against the English front. The Imperial Guard—his only reserve, and which as yet had taken no part in the battle—was drawn up at seven in two huge columns of attack. The first, with Ney himself at its head, swept all before it as it mounted the rise beside La Haye Sainte, on which the thin English line still held its ground, and all but touched the English front when its mass, torn by the terrible fire of musketry with which it was received, gave way before a charge. The second, three thousand strong, advanced with the same courage over the slope near Hougomont, only to be repulsed and shattered in its turn. At the moment when these masses fell slowly and doggedly back down the fatal rise, the Prussians pushed forward on Napoleon's right, their guns swept the road to Charleroi, and Wellington seized the moment for a general advance. From that hour all was lost. Only the Guard stood firm in the wreck of the French army; and though darkness and exhaustion checked the English in their pursuit of the broken troops as they hurried from the field, the Prussian horse continued the chase through the night.

J. R. GREEN, *History of the English People.*

## 117.** AUGUST 4, 1914.

That night brought the British declaration of war against Germany. To nearly every Englishman that came as a matter of course, and it is one of the most wonderful facts in history that the Germans were surprised by it. When Mr Britling, as a sample Englishman, had said that there would never be war between Germany and England, he had always meant that it was inconceivable to him that Germany should ever attack Belgium or France. If Germany had been content to fight a merely defensive war upon her western frontier and let Belgium alone, there would hardly have been such a thing as a war party in Great Britain. But the attack upon Belgium, the westward thrust, made the whole nation flame unanimously into war. It settled a question that was in open debate up to the very outbreak of the conflict. Up to the last the English had cherished the idea that in Germany, just as in England, the mass of people were kindly, pacific, and detached. That had been the English mistake. Germany was really and truly what Germany had been professing to be for forty years, a War State. With a sigh—and a long-forgotten thrill—England roused herself to fight. Even now she still roused herself sluggishly. It was going to be an immense thing, but just how immense it was going to be no one in England had yet imagined.

Countless men that day whom Fate had marked for death and wounds stared open-mouthed at the news, and smiled with the excitement of the headlines, not dreaming that any of these things would come within three hundred miles of them.

H. G. WELLS, *Mr Britling sees it through.*

## V. CHARACTERS

### 118.* CHARITY.

It is impossible to describe with what an air of triumph my friend marched off with his new purchase; he assured me that he was firmly of opinion that those fellows must have stolen who could thus afford to sell them for half value. He informed me of several different uses to which these little pieces of wood could be applied; he expatiated largely upon the savings that would result from lighting candles with a match instead of thrusting them into the fire.

I cannot tell how long this discourse might have continued, had not his attention been called off by another object more distressful than either of the former. A woman in rags, with one child in her arms, and another on her back, was attempting to sing ballads, but with such a mournful voice that it was difficult to determine whether she was singing or crying. This was more than my friend could withstand. Even in my presence, he immediately applied his hand to his pockets, in order to relieve her; but guess his confusion, when he found that he had already given away all the money he carried about him to former objects.

OLIVER GOLDSMITH.

### 119.** THE INFLUENCE OF HABIT.

A man will tell you that he has worked in a mine for forty years unhurt by an accident as a reason why he should apprehend no danger, though the roof is beginning to sink; and it is often observable that the older a man gets the more difficult it is for him to retain a believing conception of his own death.

This influence of habit was necessarily strong in a man whose life was as monotonous as Marner's—who saw no new people and heard of no new events to keep alive in him the idea of the unexpected; and it explains simply enough why his mind should be at ease though he had left his house and his treasure more defenceless than usual. Silas was thinking with double complacency of his supper : first, because it would be hot and savoury; and secondly, because it would cost him nothing. For the little bit of pork was a present from a good housewife to whom he had this day carried home a handsome piece of linen.

GEORGE ELIOT, Silas Marner.

### 120.* SIR ROGER AT CHURCH.

As soon as the sermon is finished, nobody presumes to stir till Sir Roger is gone out of the church. The knight walks from his seat in the chancel between a double row of his tenants, that stand bowing to him on each side; and every now and then enquires how such an one's wife, or mother, or son. or father do, whom he does not see at church; which is understood as a secret reprimand to the person that is absent.

The chaplain has often told me that, upon a catechizing day, when Sir Roger has been pleased with a boy that answers well, he has ordered a bible to be given him next day for his encouragement; and sometimes accompanies it with a flitch of bacon to his mother. Sir Roger has likewise added five pounds a year to the clerk's place; and that he may encourage the young fellows to make themselves perfect in the church-service, has promised upon the death of the present incumbent, who is very old, to bestow it according to merit.

JOSEPH ADDISON, *The Spectator*.

### 121.* A SON'S GRIEF.

You will conceive my sorrow for the loss of my mother, of the best mother. If she were to live again, surely I should behave better to her. But she is happy, and what is past is nothing to her; and for me, since I cannot repair my faults to her, I hope repentance will efface them. I return you and all those that have been good to her my sincerest thanks, and pray God to repay you all with infinite advantage. Write to me and comfort me, dear child. I shall be glad likewise, if Kitty will write to me. I shall send a bill of twenty pounds in a few days, which I thought to have brought to my mother; but God suffered it not. I have not power or composure to say much more. God bless you, and bless us all.

SAMUEL JOHNSON, *Letter to Miss Porter*, 23 Jan. 1759.

### 122.** A DEVOTED WIFE.

I was guided in my choice only by the blind affection of my youth. I found an intelligent companion and a tender friend, a prudent monitress, the most faithful of wives, and a mother as tender as children ever had the misfortune to lose. I met a woman who, by the tender management of my weaknesses, gradually corrected the most pernicious of them. She became prudent from affection; and though of the most generous nature, she was taught economy and frugality by her love for me. During the most critical period of my life she preserved order in my affairs, from the care of which she relieved me.

She gently reclaimed me from dissipation; she propped my weak and irresolute nature; she urged my indolence to all the exertions that have been useful or creditable to me; and she was perpetually at hand to admonish my heedlessness and improvidence. To her I owe whatever I am; to her whatever I shall be. In her solicitude for my interest, she never for a moment forgot my feelings or my character. Even in her occasional resentment, for which I but too often gave her cause (would to God I could recall those moments!), she had no sullenness or acrimony. Her feelings were warm and impetuous; but she was placable, tender and constant. Such was she whom I have lost....I lost her, alas! (the choice of my youth and the partner of my misfortunes) at a moment when I had the prospect of her sharing my better days.

Sir JAMES MACKINTOSH, Memoirs.

123.** JOAN OF ARC.

When the thunders of universal France, as even yet may happen, shall proclaim the grandeur of the poor shepherd girl that gave up all for her country, thy ear, young shepherd girl, will have been deaf for five centuries. To suffer and to do, that was thy portion in this life; that was thy destiny; and not for a moment was it hidden from thyself. Life, thou saidst, is short; and the sleep which is in the grave is long; let me use that life, so transitory, for the glory of those heavenly dreams destined to comfort the sleep which is so long!

Never once did this holy child, as regarded herself, relax from her belief in the darkness that was travelling to meet her. She might not prefigure the very manner of her death; she saw not in vision, perhaps, the aerial altitude of the fiery scaffold, the spectators without end on every road pouring into Rouen as to a coronation, the surging smoke, the volleying flames, the hostile faces all around, the pitying eye that lurked but here and there, until nature and imperishable truth broke loose from artificial restraints;—these might not be apparent through the mists of the hurrying future. But the voice that called her to death, *that* she heard for ever.

THOMAS DE QUINCEY, Biographies.

### 124.*** CROMWELL.

Your Cromwell, what good could it do him to be "noticed" by noisy crowds of people? God his Maker already noticed him. He, Cromwell, was already there; no notice would make *him* other than he already was. Till his hair was grown gray, and Life from the downhill slope was all seen to be limited, not infinite but finite, and all a measurable matter *how* it went,— he had been content to plow the ground, and read his Bible. He in his old days could not support it any longer, without selling himself to Falsehood, that he might ride in gilt carriages to Whitehall, and have clerks with bundles of papers haunting him, "Decide this, decide that," which in utmost sorrow of heart no man can perfectly decide.! What could gilt carriages do for this man? From of old, was there not in his life a weight of meaning, a terror, and a splendour as of Heaven itself? His existence there as man set him beyond the need of gilding Death, Judgment and Eternity; these already lay as the background of whatsoever he thought or did. All his life lay begirt as in a sea of nameless Thoughts, which no speech of a mortal could name. God's Word, as the Puritan prophets of that time had read it; this was great, and all else was little to him. To call such a man "ambitious," to figure him as the prurient windbag described above, seems to me the poorest solecism. Such a man will say: "Keep your gilt carriages and huzzaing mob; keep your red-tape clerks, your influentialities, your important businesses. Leave me alone, leave me alone; there is too much of life in me already!"     THOMAS CARLYLE.

### 125.* WILLIAM OF ORANGE.

The king meanwhile was sinking fast. Albemarle had arrived at Kensington from the Hague, exhausted by rapid travelling. His master kindly bade him go to rest for some hours, and then summoned him to make his report. That report was in all respects satisfactory. The States General were in the best temper; the troops were in the best order. Everything was in readiness for an early campaign. William received the intelligence with the calmness of a man whose work was done. " I am fast drawing," he said, " to my end." His end was worthy of his life. His intellect was not for a moment clouded. He had very lately said to one of those whom he most loved : " You know that I never feared death ; there have been times when I should have wished it ; but now that this great new prospect is opening before me, I do wish to stay here a little longer." Yet no weakness disgraced the close of that noble career.

Lord MACAULAY, History of England.

## 126.** GEORGE THE THIRD AT HOME.

King George's household was a model of an English gentleman's household. It was early; it was kindly; it was charitable; it was frugal; it was orderly; it must have been stupid to a degree which I shudder now to contemplate. No wonder all the Princes ran away from the lap of that dreary domestic virtue. It always rose, rode, dined at stated intervals. Day after day was the same. At the same hour at night the King kissed his daughters' jolly cheeks ; the Princesses kissed their mother's hand ; and Madame Thielke brought the Royal nightcap. At the same hour the equerries and women-in-waiting had their little dinner, and cackled over their tea. The King had his backgammon or his evening concert ; the equerries yawned themselves to death in the anteroom ; or the King and his family walked on Windsor slopes, the King holding his darling little Princess Amelia by the hand ; and the people crowded round quite good-naturedly; and the Eton boys thrust their chubby cheeks under the crowd's elbows ; and the concert over, the King never failed to take his enormous cocked-hat off, and salute his band, and say, "Thank you, gentlemen."

W. M. THACKERAY, Lectures on The Four Georges.

6—2

## 127.** NELSON.

The death of Nelson was felt in England as something more than a public calamity : men started at the intelligence, and turned pale, as if they had heard of the loss of a dear friend. An object of our admiration and affection, of our pride and of our hopes, was suddenly taken from us; and it seemed as if we had never till then known how deeply we loved and reverenced him. What the country had lost in its great naval hero—the greatest of our own and of all former times—was scarcely taken into the account of grief.

So perfectly indeed had he performed his part, that the maritime war, after the battle of Trafalgar, was considered at an end : the fleets of the enemy were not merely defeated, but destroyed ; new navies must be built, and a new race of seamen reared for them, before the possibility of their invading our shores could again be contemplated. It was not, therefore, from any selfish reflexion upon the magnitude of our loss that we mourned for him; the general sorrow was of a higher character.

The people of England grieved that funeral ceremonies, public monuments, and posthumous rewards were all which they could now bestow upon him whom the king, the legislature, and the nation, would alike have delighted to honour; whom every tongue would have blessed; whose presence in every village through which he might have passed would have waked the church bells, have given school-boys a holiday, have drawn children from their sports to gaze upon him, and "old men from the chimney corner" to look upon Nelson ere they died.                ROBERT SOUTHEY, *Life of Nelson.*

## 128.** NAPOLEON AT ST HELENA.

With his restless energy thrown back on himself, Napoleon was devoured by his inverted activities. He could not exist except in a stress of work. Work, he said, was his element ; he was born and made for work. He had known, he would say, the limits of his powers of walking or of seeing, but had never been able to ascertain the limits of his power of work. His mind and body, says Chaptal, were incapable of fatigue.

How was employment to be found at Longwood for this formidable machine? The powers of brain and nerve and body which had grappled with the world now turned on him and rent him. To learn enough English to read in the newspapers what was going on in the Europe which he had controlled, to dictate memoirs giving his point of view of what interested him at the moment, to gossip about his custodians, to preserve order and harmony in his little household,—these were the crumbs of existence which he was left to mumble. There is no parallel to his position. The world has usually made short work of its Cæsars when it has done with them. Napoleon had sought death in battle, and by suicide, in vain. The constant efforts of assassination had been fruitless. The hopes of our Ministers that the French Government would shoot or hang him had been disappointed. So Europe buckled itself to the unprecedented task of gagging and paralysing an intelligence and a force which were too gigantic for the welfare and security of the world. That is the strange, unique, hideous problem which makes the records of St Helena so profoundly painful and fascinating.

The Earl of ROSEBERY, *Napoleon: the Last Phase.*

### 129.** SCOTT'S "FAITHLESSNESS."

Thus, the most startling fault of the age being its faithlessness, it is necessary that its greatest man should be faithless. Nothing is more notable or sorrowful in Scott's mind than its incapacity of steady belief in anything. He cannot even resolve hardily to believe in a ghost, or a water-spirit; always explains them away in an apologetic manner, not believing, all the while, even in his own explanation. He never can clearly ascertain whether there is anything behind the arras but rats; never draws sword, and thrusts at it for life or death; but goes on looking at it timidly, and saying, "It must be the wind." He is educated a Presbyterian, and remains one, because it is the most sensible thing he can do if he is to live in Edinburgh;

but he thinks Romanism more picturesque, and profaneness more gentlemanly; does not see that anything affects human life but love, courage, and destiny; which are, indeed, not matters of faith at all, but of sight. Any gods but those are very misty in outline to him; and when the love is laid ghastly in poor Charlotte's coffin; and the courage is no more of use, —the pen having fallen from between the fingers; and destiny is sealing the scroll,—the God-light is dim in the tears that fall on it.

He is in all this the epitome of his epoch.

JOHN RUSKIN, *Modern Painters.*

### 130.*** FRENCH INDEPENDENCE.

At last I saw a nice old man and his wife looking at me with some interest, so I gave them good day and pulled up alongside. I began with a remark upon their dog, which had somewhat the look of a pointer; thence I slid into a compliment on Madame's flowers, and thence into a word in praise of their way of life.

If you ventured on such an experiment in England you would get a slap in the face at once. The life would be shown to be a vile one, not without a side-shot at your better fortune. Now, what I like so much in France is the clear unflinching recognition by everybody of his own luck. They all know on what side their bread is buttered, and take a pleasure in showing it to others, which is surely the better part of religion. And they scorn to make a poor mouth over their poverty, which I take to be the better part of manliness. I have heard a woman, in quite a better position at home, with a good bit of money in hand, refer to her own child with a horrid whine as "a poor man's child." I would not say such a thing to the Duke of Westminster. And the French are full of this spirit of independence. Perhaps it is the result of republican institutions, as they call them. Much more likely it is because there are so few people really poor, that the whiners are not enough to keep each other in countenance.

R. L. STEVENSON, *An Inland Voyage.*

### 131.** A Typical French Family.

The heat of the debate was rivalled outside by the torrid noonday sun blazing on the white houses of the Avenue Gambetta, deserted at this hour, whither my way took me to a modest habitation. There, in a cool apartment into which softened rays of light filtered through the shutters, the atmospheric change from the burning street without was as striking as the moral contrast of the calm of the people sitting there with the fiery uproar of the gesticulating politicians.

It was the home and workshop of a wood-carver, whose skill, famed through the region, had long ago dispensed him of the need for manual toil which he loved with the zeal of a craftsman of old. This simple provincial family composed a characteristic French group, the head of it grown gray in intelligent labour; his wife vigorous and orderly, keeping his books as well as the house; his daughter, as comely as was her mother before the War, lately married to a young cultivator of the neighbourhood, also present, who had completed his military service.

This roomful of contented people contained the materials that promote the prosperity and real glory of France—industry, thrift, family sentiment, artistic instinct, cultivation of the soil, cheerful performance of patriotic duty, and collaboration of woman in the plan of life—all impregnated with an air of the old Latin civilisation, oftener manifest in humble spheres than in the class which ought longest to have preserved it.

J. E. C. BODLEY, *France.*

### 132.* The Yeoman Soldier.

I looked fully as much at that man as at the strange place where we now were, and which was every moment becoming stranger. He was a fine specimen of the yeoman turned soldier. There he paces along, tall, strong, ruddy, and chestnut-haired, an Englishman every inch. I prize the sturdy Scot; I love the daring and impetuous Irishman; I admire all the various races which constitute the population of the British Isles; yet I must say that, upon the whole, none are so well adapted to ply the soldier's hardy trade as the rural sons of old England, —so strong, so cool, yet, at the same time, animated with so much hidden fire. Turn to the history of England, and you will at once perceive of what such men are capable; even at Hastings, in the gray old time, under almost every disadvantage, they all but vanquished the Norman chivalry. Trace their deeds in France, which they twice subdued; and even follow them to Spain, where they twanged the yew and raised the battle-axe, and left behind them a name of glory at Inglis Mendi, a name that shall last till fire consumes the Cantabrian hills. And oh, in modern times, trace the deeds of these gallant men all over the world, and especially in France and Spain, and admire them, even as I did that sober, silent, soldier-like man.                GEORGE BORROW, *The Bible in Spain.*

### 133.* AN IRISH SHEPHERD GIRL.

The only house near to her father's was that occupied by Bessie Hannigan. The other few houses were scattered widely with long, quiet miles of hill and bog between them, so that she had hardly seen more than a couple of men beside her father since she was born. She helped her father and mother in all the small businesses of their house, and every day also she drove their three cows and two goats to pasture on the mountain slopes. Here through the sunny days the years had passed in a slow, warm thoughtlessness wherein, without thinking, many thoughts had entered into her mind and many pictures hung for a moment like birds in the thin air. At first, and for a long time, she had been happy enough; there were many things in which a child might be interested: the spacious heavens which never wore the same beauty on any day; the innumerable little creatures living among the grasses or in the heather; the steep swing of a bird down from the mountain to the infinite plains below; the little flowers which were so contented each in its peaceful place; the bees gathering food for their houses, and the stout beetles who are always losing their way in the dusk. These things, and many others, interested her.                JAMES STEPHENS, *The Crock of Gold.*

### 134.* THE PUBLIC SCHOOL MANNER.

The walk through the flat Cambridgeshire country was long and strenuous; though for at least half of it the active journalist who was Ashe's companion conceived the poorest opinion of the new Minister. Ashe knew nothing; had no opinions; cared for nothing, except now and then for the stalking of an unfamiliar bird, or the antics of the dogs, or tales of horse-racing, of which he talked with a fervour entirely denied to those high political topics of which Kershaw's ardent soul was full.

Again and again did the journalist put them under his nose in their most attractive guise. In vain; Ashe would have none of them, till suddenly a chance word started an Indian frontier question, vastly important, and totally unknown to the English public. Ashe casually began to talk; the trickle became a stream, and presently he was holding forth with an impetuosity, a knowledge, a matured and careful judgment that fairly amazed the man beside him.

The long road, bordered by the flat fen meadows, the wide silver sky, the gently lengthening day, all passed unnoticed. The journalist found himself in the grip of a *mind*—strong, active, rich. He gave himself up with docility, yet with a growing astonishment; and when they stood once more on the steps of the house, he said to his companion,—

"You must have followed these matters for years. Why have you never spoken in the House, or written anything?"

Ashe's aspect changed at once.

"What would have been the good?" he said, with his easy smile. "The fellows who didn't know wouldn't have believed me; and the fellows who knew didn't want telling."

Mrs HUMPHRY WARD, *The Marriage of William Ashe.*

### 135.** THE EDUCATION OF MR POLLY.

Mr Polly went into the National School at six, and he left the private school at fourteen, and by that time...he had lost much of his natural confidence, so far as figures and sciences and languages and the possibilities of learning things were concerned. He thought of the present world no longer as a wonderland of experiences, but as geography and history, as the repeating of names that were hard to pronounce, and lists of products and populations and heights and lengths, and as lists and dates—oh! and Boredom indescribable.

He thought of religion as the recital of more or less incomprehensible words that were hard to remember, and of the Divinity as of a limitless Being having the nature of a schoolmaster and making infinite rules, known and unknown, rules that were always ruthlessly enforced, and with an infinite capacity for punishment, and, most horrible of all to think of, limitless powers of espial. (So to the best of his ability he did not think of that unrelenting eye.)

He was uncertain about the spelling and pronunciation of most of the words in our beautiful but abundant and perplexing tongue—that especially was a pity, because words attracted him, and under happier conditions he might have used them well—he was always doubtful whether it was eight sevens or nine eights that was sixty-three (he knew no method for settling the difficulty), and he thought the merit of a drawing consisted in the care with which it was "lined in." "Lining in" bored him beyond measure.

H. G. WELLS, *The History of Mr Polly.*

## VI. CONVERSATIONAL

### 136.* DISCOURSE WITH CHARITY.

Then said Charity to Christian, Have you a family? are you a married man?

CHR. I have a wife and four small children.

CHAR. And why did you not bring them along with you?

Then Christian wept, and said, Oh, how willingly would I have done it! but they were all of them utterly averse to my going on pilgrimage.

CHAR. But you should have talked to them, and have endeavoured to have shown them the danger of staying behind.

CHR. So I did; and told them also what God had shown to me of the destruction of our city; but I seemed to them as one that mocked, and they believed me not.

CHAR. And did you pray to God that he would bless your counsel to them?

CHR. Yes, and that with much affection; for you must think that my wife and poor children were very dear unto me.

CHAR. But did you tell them of your own sorrow, and fear of destruction? for I suppose that destruction was visible enough to you.

CHR. Yes, over, and over, and over. They might also see my fears in my countenance, in my tears, and also in my trembling under the apprehension of the judgment that did hang over our heads; but all was not sufficient to prevail with them to come with me.

CHAR. But what could they say for themselves why they came not?

CHR. Why, my wife was afraid of losing this world, and my children were given to the foolish delights of youth; so, what by one thing, and what by another, they left me to wander in this manner alone.

JOHN BUNYAN, *The Pilgrim's Progress.*


## 137.** A BRAID OF HAIR.

"What colour might the braid of hair be that thou pratest of?"

Varney replied, "A poet, Madam, might call it a thread from the golden web wrought by Minerva; but, to my thinking, it was paler than even the purest gold—more like the last parting sunbeam of the softest day of spring."

"Why, you are a poet yourself, Master Varney," said the Queen, smiling; "but I have not genius quick enough to follow your rare metaphors—Look round these ladies—is there (she hesitated, and endeavoured to assume an air of great indifference)—Is there here, in this presence, any lady, the colour of whose hair reminds thee of that braid? Methinks, without prying into my Lord of Leicester's amorous secrets, I would fain know what kind of locks are like the thread of

Minerva's web, or the—what was it?—the last rays of the May-day sun."

Varney looked round in the presence-chamber, his eye travelling from one lady to another, until at length it rested upon the Queen herself, but with an aspect of the deepest veneration, "I see no tresses," he said, "in this presence worthy of such similes, unless where I dare not look on them."

Sir WALTER SCOTT, Kenilworth.

### 138.** THE HIGH ROAD TO ENGLAND.

Mr Davies mentioned my name, and respectfully introduced me to him. I was much agitated; and recollecting his prejudice against the Scotch, of which I had heard much, I said to Davies, "Don't tell where I come from." "From Scotland," cried Davies roguishly. "Mr Johnson (said I), I do indeed come from Scotland, but I cannot help it."

I am willing to flatter myself that I meant this as light pleasantry to soothe and conciliate him, and not as any humiliating abasement at the expense of my country. But however that might be, this speech was somewhat unlucky; for with that quickness of wit for which he was so remarkable, he seized the expression "come from Scotland," which I used in the sense of being of that country, and, as if I had said that I had come away from it, or left it, retorted, "That, sir, I find, is what a very great many of your countrymen cannot help."

This stroke stunned me a good deal; and when we had sat down I felt myself not a little embarrassed and apprehensive of what might come next.

JAMES BOSWELL, Life of Dr Johnson.

### 139.** AN IMAGINARY CONVERSATION.

HOME. I hope, sir, our mountains will detain you among them some time, and I presume to promise you that you will find in Edinburgh a society as polished and literate as in Paris.

HUME. As literate I can easily believe, my cousin, and perhaps as polished, if you reason upon the ingredients of polish; but there is certainly much more amenity and urbanity at Paris than anywhere else in the world, and people there are less likely to give and take offence. All topics may be discussed without arrogance and superciliousness; an atheist would see you worship a stool or light a candle at noon without a sneer at you; and a bishop, if you were well dressed and perfumed, would argue with you calmly and serenely, though you doubted the whole Athanasian creed.

HOME. So much the worse: God forbid we should ever experience this lukewarmness in Scotland!

HUME. God, it appears, has forbidden it; for which reason, to show my obedience and submission, I live as much as possible in France, where at present God has forbidden no such thing.

HOME. Religion, my dear sir, can alone make men happy and keep them so.

HUME. Nothing is better calculated to make men happy than religion, if you will allow them to manage it according to their minds; in which case the strong men hunt down others till they can fold them, entrap them, or noose them. Here, however, let the discussion terminate.

WALTER SAVAGE LANDOR,
*Imaginary Conversations* (*David Hume and John Home*).

### 140.* IN A DRAWING-ROOM.

Such was the conversation till tea-time, when the appearance of Mr Smith gave a new turn to the discourse.

Miss Branghton desired me to remark with what a smart air he entered the room, and asked me if he had not very much a quality look?

"Come," cried he, advancing to us, "you ladies must not sit together; wherever I go, I always make it a rule to part the ladies."

And then, handing Miss Branghton to the next chair, he seated himself between us.

"Well, now, ladies, I think we sit very well. What say you? For my part, I think it was a very good motion."

"If my cousin likes it," said Miss Branghton, "I'm sure I've no objection."

"O," cried he, "I always study what the ladies like—that's my first thought. And, indeed, it is but natural that you should like best to sit by the gentlemen, for what can you find to say to one another?"

"Say!" cried young Branghton; "O, never you think of that, they'll find enough to say, I'll be sworn. You know the women are never tired of talking."

"Come, come, Tom," said Mr Smith, "don't be severe upon the ladies; when I'm by, you know I always take their part."

FRANCES BURNEY (Madame D'ARBLAY), *Evelina*.

### 141.* ON BREAKING UP A PARTY.

"You will make my excuses, my dear, as civilly as possible. You will say that I am quite an invalid, and go nowhere, and therefore must decline her obliging invitation; beginning with my *compliments*, of course. But you will do everything right. I need not tell you what is to be done. We must remember to let James know the carriage will be wanted on Tuesday. I shall have no fears for you with him. We have never been there above once since the new approach was made; but still I have no doubt that James will take you very safely; and when you get there you must tell him at what time you would have him come for you again; and you had better name an early hour. You will not like staying late. You will get very tired when tea is over."

"But you would not wish me to come away before I am tired, papa?"

"Oh no, my love; but you will soon be tired. There will be a great many people talking at once. You will not like the noise."

"But, my dear sir," cried Mr Weston, "if Emma comes away early it will be breaking up the party."

"And no great harm if it does," said Mr Woodhouse. "The sooner every party breaks up the better."

JANE AUSTEN, *Emma*.

### 142.* STARTLING ALACRITY.

The evening of the day on which we heard of Mr Holbrook's death, Miss Matilda was very silent and thoughtful; after prayers she called Martha back, and then she stood uncertain what to say.

"Martha!" she said at last; "you are young,"—and then she made so long a pause that Martha, to remind her of her half-finished sentence, dropped a courtesy, and said—"Yes, please, ma'am; two-and-twenty last third of October, please, ma'am."

"And perhaps, Martha, you may some time meet with a young man you like, and who likes you. I did say you were not to have followers; but if you meet with such a young man, and tell me, and I find he is respectable, I have no objection to his coming to see you once a week. God forbid!" said she, in a low voice, "that I should grieve any young hearts." She spoke as if she were providing for some distant contingency, and was rather startled when Martha made her ready eager answer:

"Please, ma'am, there's Jim Hearn, and he's a joiner, making three-and-sixpence a day, and six foot one in his stocking-feet, please, ma'am; and if you'll ask about him to-morrow morning, everyone will give him a character for steadiness; and he'll be glad enough to come to-morrow night, I'll be bound."

Mrs GASKELL, *Cranford.*

### 143.* AN ERROR EXPLAINED.

"I find I have done you a wrong, Colonel Washington," George said, "and must apologise, not for the error, but for much of my late behaviour which has resulted from it."

"The error was mine! It was I who found that paper in your room, and showed it to George, and was jealous of you, Colonel," cried Mrs Mountain.

"'Tis a pity you could not have kept your eyes off my paper, madam," said Mr Washington. "You will permit me to say so. A great deal of mischief has come because I chose to keep a secret which concerned only myself and another person. For a long time George Warrington's heart has been black with anger against me, and my feeling towards him has, I own, scarce been more friendly. All this pain might have been spared to both of us, had my private papers only been read by those for whom they were written. I shall say no more now, lest my feelings again should betray me into hasty words. Heaven bless thee, Harry! Farewell, George! And take a true friend's advice, and try and be less ready to think evil of your friends. We shall meet again at the camp, and will keep our weapons for the enemy."

W. M. THACKERAY, The Virginians.

### 144.** THE HISTORICAL BLOOD-STAIN.

Suddenly Mrs Otis caught sight of a dull red stain on the floor just by the fireplace and, quite unconscious of what it really signified, said to Mrs Umney, "I am afraid something has been spilt there."

"Yes, madam," replied the old housekeeper in a low voice, "blood has been spilt on that spot."

"How horrid," cried Mrs Otis; "I don't at all care for blood-stains in a sitting-room. It must be removed at once."

The old woman smiled, and answered in the same low, mysterious voice, "It is the blood of Lady Eleanore de Canterville, who was murdered on that very spot by her own husband, Sir Simon de Canterville, in 1575. Sir Simon survived her nine years, and disappeared suddenly under very mysterious circumstances. His body has never been discovered, but his guilty spirit still haunts the Chase. The blood-stain has been much admired by tourists and others, and cannot be removed."

"That is all nonsense," cried Washington Otis; "Pinkerton's Champion Stain Remover and Paragon Detergent will clean it up in no time," and before the terrified housekeeper could interfere he had fallen upon his knees, and was rapidly scouring the floor with a small stick of what looked like a black cosmetic. In a few moments no trace of the blood-stain could be seen.

"I knew Pinkerton would do it," he exclaimed triumphantly, as he looked round at his admiring family; but no sooner had he said these words than a terrible flash of lightning lit up the sombre room, a fearful peal of thunder made them all start to their feet, and Mrs Umney fainted.

"What a monstrous climate!" said the American Minister calmly, as he lit a long cheroot. "I guess the old country is so overpopulated that they have not enough decent weather for everybody. I have always been of opinion that emigration is the only thing for England."

"My dear Hiram," cried Mrs Otis, "what can we do with a woman who faints?"

"Charge it to her like breakages," answered the Minister; "she won't faint after that"; and in a few moments Mrs Umney certainly came to.

OSCAR WILDE, The Canterville Ghost.

### 145.* THE PHILOSOPHER RESOLVES TO DIE.

When the children were ten years of age, one of the Philosophers died. He called the household together and announced that the time had come when he must bid them all good-bye, and that his intention was to die as quickly as might be....

The other Philosopher replied mildly as he lit his pipe:

"Brother, the greatest of all virtues is curiosity, and the end of all desire is wisdom; tell us, therefore, by what steps you have arrived at this commendable resolution."

To this the Philosopher replied:

"I have attained to all the wisdom which I am fitted to bear. In the space of one week no new truth has come to me. All that I have read lately I knew before; all that I have thought has been but a recapitulation of old and wearisome ideas. There is no longer an horizon before my eyes. Space has narrowed to the petty dimensions of my thumb. Time is the tick of a clock. Good and evil are two peas in the one pod. My wife's face is the same for ever. I want to play with the children, and yet 1 do not want to. Your conversation with me,

brother, is like the droning of a bee in a dark cell. The pine
trees take root and grow and die.—It's all bosh. Good-bye."

JAMES STEPHENS, The Crock of Gold.

**146.\*  THE PHILOSOPHER RESOLVES TO DIE (*continued*).**

His friend replied:

"Brother, these are weighty reflections, and I do clearly
perceive that the time has come for you to stop. I might
observe, not in order to combat your views, but merely to
continue an interesting conversation, that there are still some
knowledges which you have not assimilated—you do not yet
know how to play the tambourine, nor how to be nice to your
wife, nor how to get up first in the morning and cook the
breakfast. Have you learned how to smoke strong tobacco as
I do? or can you dance in the moonlight with a woman of
the Shee? To understand the theory which underlies all things
is not sufficient. Theory is but the preparation for practice.
It has occurred to me, brother, that wisdom may not be the
end of everything. Goodness and kindliness are, perhaps,
beyond wisdom. Is it not possible that the ultimate end is
gaiety and music and a dance of joy? Wisdom is the oldest
of all things. Wisdom is all head and no heart. Behold, brother, you are being crushed under the weight of your head.
You are dying of old age while you are yet a child."

"Brother," replied the other Philosopher, "your voice is like
the droning of a bee in a dark cell. If in my latter days I am
reduced to playing on the tambourine and running after a
hag in the moonlight, and cooking your breakfast in the grey
morning, then it is indeed time that I should die. Good-bye,
brother."

JAMES STEPHENS, The Crock of Gold.

**147.\*  THE CROCK OF GOLD.**

"You say that this unhealthy woman has not got your
wife's washboard. It remains, therefore, that the fairies have
it."

"It looks that way," said Meehawl.

" There are six clans of fairies living in this neighbourhood;
but the process of elimination which has shaped the world to
a globe, the ant to its environment, and man to the captaincy
of the vertebrates, will not fail in this instance either."

"Did you ever see anything like the way wasps have increased this season," said Meehawl; "faith, you can't sit down
anywhere but your breeches— "

"I did not," said the Philosopher. "Did you leave out a pan
of milk on last Tuesday?"

"I did then...."

"Did you cut down a thorn-bush recently?"

"I'd sooner cut my eye out," said Meehawl, "and go about
as wall-eyed as Lorcan O'Nualain's ass: I would that. Did
you ever see his ass, sir? It— "

"I did not," said the Philosopher. "Did you kill a robin
redbreast?"

"Never," said Meehawl. "By the pipers," he added, "that
old skinny cat of mine caught a bird on the roof yesterday."

"Hah!" cried the Philosopher, moving, if it were possible,
even closer to his client, "now we have it. It is the Leprecauns
of Gort na Cloca Mora took your washboard. Go to the Gort
at once. There is a hole under a tree in the south-east of the
field. Try what you will find in that hole."

"I'll do that," said Meehawl. "Did you ever— "

"I did not," said the Philosopher.

So Meehawl MacMurrachu went away and did as he had
been bidden, and underneath the tree of Gort na Cloca Mora
he found a little crock of gold.

"There's a power of washboards in that," said he.

JAMES STEPHENS, *The Crock of Gold.*


148.** THE PHILOSOPHER AT THE POLICE BARRACKS.

"I want to give myself up," said the Philosopher.
The policeman looked at him—

"A man as old as you are," said he, "oughtn't to be a fool.
Go home now, I advise you, and don't say a word to anyone

whether you did it or not. Tell me this now, was it found out, or are you only making a clean breast of it?"

"Sure I must give myself up," said the Philosopher

"If you must, you must, and that's an end of it. Wipe your feet on the rail there and come in—I'll take your deposition."

"I have no deposition for you," said the Philosopher, "for I didn't do a thing at all."

The policeman stared at him again.

"If that's so," said he, "you needn't come in at all, and you needn't have wakened me out of my sleep either. Maybe, tho', you are the man that fought the badger on the Naas Road—Eh?"

"I am not," replied the Philosopher: "but I was arrested for killing my brother and his wife, although I never touched them."

"Is that who you are?" said the policeman; and then, briskly, "You're as welcome as the cuckoo, you are so. Come in and make yourself comfortable till the men awaken, and they are the lads that'll be glad to see you."

JAMES STEPHENS, *The Crock of Gold.*

### 149.** REPORT OF AN INTERVIEW.

My guardian called me into his room next morning, and then I told him what had been left untold on the previous night. There was nothing to be done, he said, but to keep the secret, and to avoid another such encounter as that of yesterday. He understood my feeling, and entirely shared it. He charged himself even with restraining Mr Skimpole from improving his opportunity. One person, whom he need not name to me, it was not now possible for him to advise or help. He wished it were; but no such thing could be. If her mistrust of the lawyer whom she had mentioned were well founded, which he scarcely doubted, he dreaded discovery. He knew something of him, both by sight and by reputation, and it was certain that he was a dangerous man. Whatever happened, he repeatedly pressed upon me with anxious affection and kindness, I was as innocent of as himself; and as unable to influence.    DICKENS, *Bleak House.*

## VII. LANGUAGE AND LITERATURE

### 150.*** OF STUDIES.

Read not to contradict and confute ; nor to believe and take
for granted ; nor to find talk and discourse ; but to weigh and
consider. Some books are to be tasted, others to be swallowed,
and some few to be chewed and digested ; that is, some books
are to be read only in parts; others to be read, but not curiously ; and some few to be read wholly, and with diligence
and attention. Some books may also be read by deputy, and
extracts made of them by others; but that would be only in the
less important arguments, and the meaner sort of books ; else
distilled books are like common distilled waters, flashy things.
Reading maketh a full man ; conference a ready man ; and
writing an exact man. And therefore, if a man write little, he
had need have a great memory ; if he confer little, he had
need have a present wit : and if he read little, he had need
have much cunning, to seem to know that he doth not. His-
tories make men wise ; poets witty ; the mathematics subtle ;
natural philosophy deep ; moral grave ; logic and rhetoric
able to contend. *Abeunt studia in mores.*

FRANCIS BACON, Essays.

### 151.*** THE CENSORSHIP OF THE PRESS.

I deny not but that it is of greatest concernment in the
church and commonwealth, to have a vigilant eye how books
demean themselves, as well as men ; and thereafter to confine,
imprison, and do sharpest justice on them as malefactors ; for
books are not absolutely dead things, but do contain a potency
of life in them to be as active as that soul was whose progeny
they are ; nay, they do preserve as in a vial the purest efficacy
and extraction of that living intellect that bred them. I know
they are as lively, and as vigorously productive, as those fabulous dragon's teeth : and being sown up and down, may chance
to spring up armed men.

And yet, on the other hand, unless wariness be used, as good almost kill a man as kill a good book: who kills a man kills a reasonable creature, God's image; but he who destroys a good book kills reason itself, kills the image of God, as it were, in the eye. Many a man lives a burden to the earth; but a good book is the precious life-blood of a master spirit, embalmed and treasured up on purpose to a life beyond life.

JOHN MILTON, *Areopagitica.*

### 152.\* READING AND TIME.

The most illusory of all the work that we propose to ourselves is reading. It seems so easy to read, that we intend, in the indefinite future, to master the vastest literatures. We cannot bring ourselves to admit that the library we have collected is in great part closed to us simply by want of time. A dear friend of mine, who was a solicitor with a large practice, indulged in wonderful illusions about reading, and collected several thousand volumes, all fine editions, but he died without having cut their leaves.

I like the university habit of making reading a business, and estimating the mastery of a few authors as a just title to consideration for scholarship. I should like very well to be shut up in a garden for a whole summer with no literature but the "Faëry Queene," and one year I very nearly realized that project, but publishers and the postman interfered with it.

After all, this business of reading ought to be less illusory than most others, for printers divide books into pages, which they number, so that, with a moderate skill in arithmetic, one ought to be able to foresee the limits of his possibilities.

P. G. HAMERTON, *The Intellectual Life.*

### 153.\*\* LOSS OF INTEREST IN BOOKS.

Literature, its exertions and objects, were now of little moment in my regard. I cared not at this period for books; they were apart from me. Nature—except it were human nature—the nature that is developed in earth and sky, was,

in one sense, hidden from me ; and all the imaginative delight
wherewith it had been spiritualised passed away out of my
mind.  A gift, a faculty, if it had not departed, was suspended
and inanimate within me.  There would have been something
sad, unutterably dreary, in all this, had I not been conscious
that it lay at my own option to recall whatever was valuable
in the past.  It might be true, indeed, that this was a life
which could not, with impunity, be lived too long ; else it
might make me permanently other than I had been, without
transforming me into any shape which it would be worth my
while to take.  But I never considered it as other than a transitory life.  There was always a prophetic instinct, a low whisper
in my ear, that within no long period, and whenever a new
change of custom should be essential to my good, change
would come.

NATHANIEL HAWTHORNE, *The Scarlet Letter.*

### 154.*** THE VALUE OF BOOKS.

A precious thing is all the more precious to us if it has been
won by work or economy ; and if public libraries were half as
costly as public dinners, or books cost the tenth part of what
bracelets do, even foolish men and women might sometimes
suspect there was good in reading, as well as in munching
and sparkling ; whereas the very cheapness of literature is
making even wise people forget that if a book is worth reading, it is worth buying.  No book is worth anything which is
not worth *much* ; nor is it serviceable, until it has been read,
and re-read, and loved, and loved again ; and marked, so that
you can refer to the passages you want in it, as a soldier can
seize the weapon he needs in an armoury, or a housewife bring
the spice she needs from her store.  Bread of flour is good ;
but there is bread, sweet as honey, if we would eat it, in a
good book ; and the family must be poor indeed which, once
in their lives, cannot, for such multipliable barley-loaves, pay
their baker's bill.  We call ourselves a rich nation, and we are
filthy and foolish enough to thumb each other's books out of
circulating libraries !    JOHN RUSKIN, *Sesame and Lilies.*

### 155.*** Why Great Literature is Immortal.

Let us consider, too, how differently young and old are affected by the words of some classic author, such as Homer or Horace. Passages, which to a boy are but rhetorical commonplaces, neither better nor worse than a hundred others which any clever writer might supply, which he gets by heart and thinks very fine, and imitates, as he thinks, successfully, in his own flowing versification, at length comes home to him, when long years have passed, and he has had experience of life, and pierce him, as if he had never before known them, with their sad earnestness and vivid exactness.

Then he comes to understand how it is that lines, the birth of some chance morning or evening at an Ionian festival, or among the Sabine hills, have lasted generation after generation, for thousands of years, with a power over the mind, and a charm, which the current literature of his own day, with all its obvious advantages, is utterly unable to rival. Perhaps this is the reason of the mediæval opinion about Virgil, as if a prophet or magician; his single words and phrases, his pathetic half-lines, giving utterance, as the voice of Nature herself, to that pain and weariness, yet hope of better things, which is the experience of her children in every time.

J. H. NEWMAN, *The Grammar of Assent.*

### 156.*** The Life-giving Power of Literature.

To say that literature is the most important thing in life may sound an exaggeration to many: the truth is that only through literature does anything really live at all. It is in the great art creations that we come nearest to reality, in such persons as Falstaff, Cleopatra, Mrs Gamp, Othello, Becky Sharp, Micawber....

They are the real, living, persons in this world of shadows. When were Dickens's parents most alive—when they gave him mortal life, or when they received from him immortal existence as Mr Micawber and Mrs Nickleby? Which is the real Elizabeth for us—she of the school books or of Kenilworth? Who in history is as much alive as Falstaff, who in mere historical fact never existed? Whose are the spirits which, if we could summon them from the vasty deep of time, we would wish to appear before us? Not those that inhabited material flesh but those who, like the gods, are immortal because they had no mortal birth; not the actual men and women of documents and epitaphs but the great art-forms which are as much facts to us as the bodies of the men around us—nay, far more, for they have far more *life* in them, they are infinitely more alive than we who walk before our own funeral processions, most of us, from the end of adolescence to the grave; sleep-walkers without the joy of dreams.

E. A. GREENING LAMBORN, in *The Modern Teacher.*

## 157.** A SEVERE LITERARY TRAINING.

At school I enjoyed the inestimable advantage of a very sensible, though at the same time a very severe master....

I learnt from him that poetry, even that of the loftiest, and, seemingly, that of the wildest odes, had a logic of its own as severe as that of science, and more difficult, because more subtle, more complex, and dependent on more and more fugitive causes. In the truly great poets, he would say, there is a reason assignable, not only for every word, but for the position of every word; and I well remember that, availing himself of the synonymes to the Homer of Didymus, he made us attempt to show, with regard to each, why it would not have answered the same purpose, and wherein consisted the peculiar fitness of the word in the original text.

In our own English Compositions (at least for the last three years of our school education) he showed no mercy to phrase, metaphor, or image, unsupported by a sound sense, or where the same sense might have been conveyed with equal force and dignity in plainer words. Lute, harp, and lyre, muse, muses and inspirations, Pegasus, Parnassus, and Hippocrene, were all an abomination to him. In fancy I can almost hear him now, exclaiming, "Harp? Harp? Lyre? Pen and ink, boy, you mean! Muse, boy, muse? Your Nurse's daughter, you mean! Pierian spring! Oh aye! the cloister-pump, I suppose!"

S. T. COLERIDGE, *Biographia Literaria.*

### 158.* The End of a Long Task.

It was on the day, or rather night, of the 27th of June 1787, between the hours of eleven and twelve, that I wrote the last lines of the last page, in a summer-house in my garden. After laying down my pen, I took several turns in a berceau, or covered walk of acacias, which commands a prospect of the country, the lake and the mountains. The air was temperate, the sky was serene, the silver orb of the moon was reflected from the waters, and all nature was silent.

I will not dissemble the first emotions of joy on recovery of my freedom, and perhaps the establishment of my fame. But my pride was soon humbled, and a sober melancholy was spread over my mind, by the idea that I had taken an everlasting leave of an old and agreeable companion, and that whatsoever might be the future fate of my History, the life of the historian must be short and precarious.

EDWARD GIBBON, *Memoirs of my Life and Writings.*

### 159.* What We Think of Most We Speak of Least.

Having sat at the Club until the brawl there became intolerable to him, George had walked home, and had passed the night finishing some work on which he was employed, and to the completion of which he bent himself with all his might. The labour was done, and the night was worn away somehow, and the tardy November dawn came and looked in on the young man as he sate over his desk. In the next day's paper, or quarter's review, many of us very likely admired the work of his genius, the variety of his illustration, the fierce vigour of his satire, the depth of his reason. There was no hint in his writing of the other thoughts which occupied him, and always accompanied him in his work; a tone more melancholy than was customary, a satire more bitter and impatient than that which he afterwards showed, may have marked this period of his life to the very few persons who knew his style or his name. We have said before, could we know the man's feelings as well as the author's thoughts—how interesting most books would be!—more interesting than merry.

W. M. THACKERAY, *Pendennis.*

## 160.* FRANCE AS ENGLAND'S INTERPRETER.

Horace Walpole's love of the French language was of a peculiar kind. He loved it as having been for a century the vehicle of all the polite nothings of Europe, as the sign by which the freemasons of fashion recognised each other in every capital from Petersburg to Naples, as the language of raillery, as the language of anecdote, as the language of memoirs, as the language of correspondence.

Its higher uses he altogether disregarded. The literature of France has been to ours what Aaron was to Moses, the expositor of great truths which would else have perished for want of a voice to utter them with distinctness. The relation which existed between Mr Bentham and M. Dumont is an exact illustration of the intellectual relation in which the two countries stand to each other. The great discoveries in physics, in metaphysics, in political science, are ours. But scarcely any foreign nation except France has received them from us by direct communication. Isolated by our situation, isolated by our manners, we found truth, but we did not impart it. France has been the interpreter between England and mankind.

Lord MACAULAY, *Essays.*

## 161.** FRENCH PROSE AND ENGLISH POETRY.

How much more striking, in general, does any Englishman— of some vigour of mind, but by no means a poet—seem in his verse than in his prose! No doubt his verse suffers from the same defects which impair his prose, and he cannot express himself with real success in it, but how much more powerful a personage does he appear in it, by dint of feeling, and of originality and movement of ideas, than when he is writing prose!

With a Frenchman of like stamp, it is just the reverse: set him to write poetry, he is limited, artificial, and impotent; set him to write prose, he is free, natural, and effective. The power of French literature is in its prose-writers, the power of English literature is in its poets. Nay, many of the celebrated French poets depend wholly for their fame upon the qualities of intelligence which they exhibit,—qualities which are the distinctive support of prose; many of the celebrated English prose-writers depend wholly for their fame upon the qualities of genius and imagination which they exhibit,—qualities which are the distinctive support of poetry.

MATTHEW ARNOLD, *The Literary Influence of Academies.*

### 162.** THE SPIRIT OF OLD LITERATURES.

Once every people in the world believed that trees were divine, and could take a human or grotesque shape and dance among the shadows, and that deer, and ravens and foxes, and wolves and bears, and clouds and pools, almost all things under the sun and moon, and the sun and moon, were not less divine and changeable. They saw in the rainbow the still bent bow of a god thrown down in his negligence; they heard in the thunder the sound of his beaten war-jar, or the tumult of his chariot wheels; and when a sudden flight of wild duck, or of crows, passed over their heads, they thought they were gazing at the dead hastening to their rest, while they dreamed of so great a mystery in little things that they believed the waving of a hand, or of a sacred bough, enough to thrill far-off hearts, or hood the moon with darkness. All old literatures are full of these or of like imaginations, and all the poets of races who have not lost this way of looking at things, could have said of themselves, as the poet of the *Kalevala* said of himself, "I have learned my songs from the music of many birds, and from the music of many waters."

W. B. YEATS, *Ideas of Good and Evil.*

### 163.** THE GLORY OF THE POET.

Shakespeare wrote at a time when solitary great men were gathering to themselves the fire that had once flowed hither and thither among all men, when individualism in work and thought and emotion was breaking up the old rhythms of life, when the common people, no longer uplifted by the myths of Christianity and of still older faiths, were sinking into the earth.

The people of Stratford-on-Avon have remembered little

about him, and invented no legend to his glory. They have remembered a drinking-bout of his, and invented some bad verses for him, and that is about all. Had he been some hard-drinking, hard-living, hard-riding, loud-blaspheming Squire, they would have enlarged his fame by a legend of his dealings with the devil; but in his day the glory of a Poet, like that of all other imaginative powers, had ceased, or almost ceased outside a narrow class. The poor Gaelic rhymer leaves a nobler memory among his neighbours, who will talk of Angels standing like flames about his death-bed, and of voices speaking out of bramble-bushes that he may have the wisdom of the world. The Puritanism that drove the theatres into Surrey was but part of an inexplicable movement that was trampling out the minds of all but some few thousands born to cultivated ease.

W. B. YEATS, *Ideas of Good and Evil.*

### 164.** RESPECT FOR INTELLECT IN FRANCE.

When in England has any great man of letters been the object of popular adoration like that given to Victor Hugo and Béranger, who could hardly walk the streets of Paris without being mobbed? Where except in Paris would a taxi-driver refuse to take his fare from a great writer, saying that it was enough to have the honour of driving Anatole France? If there were an Anatole France in London no taxi-driver would know him by sight. The Parisian *midinette* makes pilgrimages to the grave of the original "Dame aux Camélias" in Montmartre cemetery and lays violets on the tomb of Abélard and Héloïse in Père-Lachaise. Nothing more endears to one the French people than their passionate cult of genius and their immense respect for intellectual superiority.

But, like all human qualities, this respect for intellect has its drawbacks; literature and men of letters have had too great an influence in France. Their influence is one of the causes of the excessive importance attached to words and to ideas in themselves. It has led to a notion that, when one has had a fine idea and has expressed it in fine language, one has done all that is necessary.

ROBERT DELL, *My Second Country (France).*

## 165.** ANDROMACHE.

One while he appeared much concerned about Andromache; and a little while after as much for Hermione; and
was extremely puzzled to think what would become of Pyrrhus.
When Sir Roger saw Andromache's obstinate refusal to her
lover's importunities, he whispered me in the ear that he was
sure she would never have him; to which he added with a more
than ordinary vehemence, "You cannot imagine, sir, what it is to
have to do with a widow." Upon Pyrrhus his threatening afterwards to leave her, the knight shook his head, and muttered to
himself, "Ay, do if you can." This part dwelt so much upon my
friend's imagination, that at the close of the third act, as I was
thinking of something else, he whispered in my ear, "These
widows, sir, are the most perverse creatures in the world. But
pray (says he), you that are a critic, is this play according to
your dramatic rules, as you call them? Should your people in
tragedy always talk to be understood? Why, there is not a
single sentence in this play that I do not know the meaning of."
...Upon Hermione's going off with a menace to Pyrrhus, the
audience gave a loud clap; to which Sir Roger added, "On
my word, a notable young baggage!"

JOSEPH ADDISON, *Spectator.*

## 166.* THE COMÉDIE FRANÇAISE.

The tradition of the House of Molière has come down
unbroken from the Grand Siècle. The comedians who to-day
play the parts of Harpagon, Argan, Agnès, or Dorine use the
same gestures and take the same position on the stage as did
Molière and Armande Béjart and the other members of the
troupe which performed before Louis XIV. In January, June
and December, the birthdays of Molière, Corneille, and Racine
are respectively kept with the representation of a masterpiece
of the hero, and of an occasional piece illustrating an episode
in his life, written by a young hand in the ever-living metre
of the seventeenth century. On Molière's day the full company
of Sociétaires and Pensionnaires appears in the "Cérémonie"
of the *Malade Imaginaire*—the same in which, on February
10, 1673, the author uttered his last word on the stage and
was carried out to die an hour later.

Yet it is not at these solemnities that is best seen the example of the Comédie Française as a stronghold and a seminary of tradition. Nothing is more consoling than to escape from the once brilliant Boulevards and Avenues of Paris, now transformed beyond recognition by the roaring and rushing inventions of the mechanical age and to take refuge in the old theatre, when at an ordinary performance a tragedy of Corneille or Racine, or a comedy of Molière holds spellbound a vast audience representing nearly every class in the nation, and calls forth its supreme hereditary instinct in things related to art.

J. E. C. BODLEY, *The Decay of Idealism in France.*

### 167.** VOLTAIRE.

The wit and the ridicule with which Voltaire attacked the dreaming scholars of his own time, can only be appreciated by those who have studied his works. Not, as some have supposed, that he used these weapons as a substitute for argument, still less that he fell into the error of making ridicule a test for truth. No one could reason more closely than Voltaire, when reasoning suited his purpose. But he had to deal with men impervious to argument; men whose inordinate reverence for antiquity had only left them two ideas, namely, that everything old is right, and that everything new is wrong. To argue against these opinions would be idle indeed ; the only other resource was, to make them ridiculous, and weaken their influence, by holding up their authors to contempt. This was one of the tasks Voltaire set himself to perform ; and he did it well.

He, therefore, used ridicule, not as the test of truth, but as the scourge of folly. And with such effect was the punishment administered, that not only did the pedants and theologians of his own time wince under the lash, but even their successors feel their ears tingle when they read his biting words ; and they revenge themselves by reviling the memory of that great writer, whose works are as a thorn in their side, and whose very name they hold in undisguised abhorrence.

HENRY THOMAS BUCKLE, *Civilization in England.*

### 168.* COLERIDGE AND SCOTT.

Dear Sir Walter Scott and myself were exact but harmonious opposites in this: that every old ruin, hill, river, or tree, called up in his mind a host of historical or biographical associations—just as a bright pan of brass, when beaten, is said to attract the swarming bees;—whereas, for myself, notwithstanding Dr Johnson, I believe I should walk over the plain of Marathon without taking more interest in it than in any other plain of similar features. Yet I receive as much pleasure in reading the account of the battle in Herodotus, as any one can.

When I am very ill indeed I can read Scott's novels, and they are almost the only books I can then *read*. I cannot at such times read the Bible; my mind reflects on it, but I can't bear the open page.

S. T. COLERIDGE, Table Talk.

### 169.*** ON SPEAKING FRENCH.

Wherever two Englishmen are speaking French to a Frenchman you may safely diagnose in the breast of one of the two humiliation, envy, ill-will, impotent rage, and a dull yearning for vengeance; and you can take it that the degree of these emotions is in exact ratio to the superiority of the other man's performance. In the breast of this other are contempt, malicious amusement, conceit, vanity, pity, and joy in ostentation; these, also, exactly commensurable with his advantage. Strange and sad that this should be so; but so it is. French brings out the worst in all of us—all, I mean, but the few, the lamentably far too few, who cannot aspire to stammer some colloquial phrases of it.

Even in Victorian days, when England was more than geographically, was psychologically an island, French made mischief among us, and was one of the Devil's favourite ways of setting brother against brother. But in those days the bitterness of the weaker brother was a little sweetened with disapproval of the stronger. To speak French fluently and idiomatically and with a good accent—or with an idiom and accent which to other rough islanders *seemed* good—was a rather suspect accomplishment, being somehow deemed incompatible with civic worth. Thus the weaker ones had not to drain the last lees of their shame, and the stronger could not wholly rejoice in their strength. But the old saving prejudice has now died out (greatly to the delight of the Devil), and there seems no chance that it will be revived.

MAX BEERBOHM, And Even Now.

## VIII. PHILOSOPHICAL AND REFLECTIVE

### 170.* THE VISION OF MIRZAH.

He then led me to the highest pinnacle of the rock, and placing me on the top of it, "Cast thy eyes eastward," said he, "and tell me what thou seest." "I see," said I, "a huge valley, and a prodigious tide of water rolling through it." "The valley that thou seest," said he, "is the vale of misery, and the tide of water that thou seest is part of the great tide of eternity." "What is the reason," said I, "that the tide I see rises out of a thick mist at one end, and again loses itself in a thick mist at the other?" "What thou seest," says he, "is that portion of eternity which is called time, measured out by the sun, and reaching from the beginning of the world to its consummation. Examine now," said he, "this sea that is thus bounded with darkness at both ends, and tell me what thou discoverest in it." "I see a bridge," said I, "standing in the midst of the tide." "That bridge thou seest," said he, "is human life; consider it attentively."　　JOSEPH ADDISON, *Spectator.*

### 171.** MEDITATION AMONG THE TOMBS.

I know that entertainments of this nature are apt to raise dark and dismal thoughts in timorous minds and gloomy imaginations; but for my own part, though I am always serious, I do not know what it is to be melancholy; and can therefore take a view of nature in her deep and solemn scenes, with the same pleasure as in her most gay and delightful ones. By these means I can improve myself with those objects which others consider with terror.

When I look upon the tombs of the great, every emotion of envy dies in me; when I read the epitaphs of the beautiful, every inordinate desire goes out; when I meet with the grief of parents upon a tombstone, my heart melts with compassion; when I see the tomb of the parents themselves, I consider the vanity of grieving for those whom we must quickly follow; when I see kings lying by those who deposed them, when I consider rival wits placed side by side, or the holy men that divided the world with their contests and disputes, I reflect with sorrow and astonishment on the little competitions, factions, and debates of mankind. When I read the several dates of the tombs, of some that died yesterday, and some six hundred years ago, I consider that great day when we shall all of us be contemporaries, and make our appearance together.             JOSEPH ADDISON, *Spectator*.

### 172.* DR JOHNSON IN IONA.

We were now treading that illustrious island, which was once the luminary of the Caledonian regions, whence savage clans and roving barbarians derived the benefits of knowledge, and the blessings of religion. To abstract the mind from all local emotion would be impossible, if it were endeavoured, and would be foolish, if it were possible. Whatever withdraws us from the power of our senses, whatever makes the past, the distant, or the future, predominate over the present, advances us in the dignity of thinking beings. Far from me, and from my friends, be such frigid philosophy as may conduct us in-different and unmoved over any ground which has been dig-nified by wisdom, bravery, or virtue. The man is little to be envied whose patriotism would not gain force upon the plain of Marathon, or whose piety would not grow warmer among the ruins of Iona.             SAMUEL JOHNSON,
*Journey to the Western Islands of Scotland.*

### 173.* THE WALLS OF BALCLUTHA.

I have seen the walls of Balclutha, but they were desolate. The fire had resounded in the halls: and the voice of the people is heard no more. The stream of Clutha was removed from its place, by the fall of the walls. The thistle shook, there, its lonely head: the moss whistled to the wind. The fox looked out from the windows, the rank grass of the wall waved round its head. Desolate is the dwelling of Moina, silence is in the house of her fathers. Raise the song of mourning, O bards! over the land of strangers. They have but fallen before us: for, one day, we must fall. Why dost thou build the hall, son of the winged days? Thou lookest from thy towers to-day; yet a few years, and the blast of the desert comes; it howls in thy empty court, and whistles round thy half-worn shield. And let the blast of thy desert come! we shall be renowned in our day! The mark of my arm shall be in battle; my name in the song of bards. Raise the song; let joy be heard in my hall!

JAMES MACPHERSON, *Ossian (Carthon).*

### 174.* THE DRUIDS' STONE.

The temples of the mighty and skilful Roman have crumbled to dust in its neighbourhood; the churches of the Arian Goth, his successor in power, have sunk beneath the earth, and are not to be found; and the mosques of the Moor, the conqueror of the Goth, where and what are they? Upon the rock, masses of hoary and vanishing ruin. Not so the Druids' stone. There it stands on the hill of winds, as strong and as freshly new as the day, perhaps thirty centuries back, when it was first raised, by means which are a mystery. Earthquakes have heaved it, but its copestone has not fallen; rain-floods have deluged it, but failed to sweep it from its station; the burning sun has flashed upon it, but neither split nor crumbled it; and Time, stern old Time, has rubbed it with his iron tooth, and with what effect let those who view it declare. He who wishes to study the literature, the learning, and the history of the ancient Celt, may glean from that blank stone the whole known amount.

GEORGE BORROW, *The Bible in Spain.*

## 175.** THE CONSOLATIONS OF OLD AGE.

We are both in the decline of life, my dear Dean, and have been some years going down the hill; let us make the passage as smooth as we can. Let us fence against physical evil by care, and the use of those means which experience must have pointed out to us; let us fence against moral evil by philosophy. We may, nay—if we will follow nature and do not work up imagination against her plainest dictates—we shall, of course, grow every year more indifferent to life, and to the affairs and interests of a system out of which we are soon to go.

This is much better than stupidity. The decay of passion strengthens philosophy, for passion may decay and stupidity not succeed. What hurt does age do us in subduing what we toil to subdue all our lives? It is now six in the morning; I recall the time—and am glad it is over—when about this hour I used to be going to bed surfeited with pleasure, or jaded with business; my head often full of schemes, and my heart as often full of anxiety. Is it a misfortune, think you, that I rise at this hour refreshed, serene, and calm; that the past and even the present affairs of life stand like objects at a distance from me, where I can keep off the disagreeable, so as not to be strongly affected by them, and from whence I can draw the others nearer to me? Passions, in their force, would bring all these, nay even future contingencies, about my ears at once, and reason would but ill defend me in the scuffle.

Lord BOLINGBROKE, *Letter to Swift.*

## 176.* THE VIRTUES OF THE YOUNG.

At night, Mr Johnson and I supped in a private room at the Turk's Head Coffee-house, in the Strand. "I encourage this house (said he), for the mistress of it is a good civil woman, and has not much business."

"Sir, I love the acquaintance of young people; because in the first place, I don't like to think myself growing old. In the next place, young acquaintances must last longest, if they do last; and then, Sir, young men have more virtue than old men; they have more generous sentiments in every respect. I love the young dogs of this age; they have more wit and humour and knowledge of life than we had; but then the dogs are not so good scholars. Sir, in my early years I read very hard. It is a sad reflection, but a true one, that I knew almost as much at eighteen as I do now. My judgment, to be sure, was not so good; but I had all the facts. I remember very well, when I was at Oxford, an old gentleman said to me, 'Young man, ply your book diligently now, and acquire a stock of knowledge; for when years come upon you, you will find that poring upon books will be but an irksome task.'"

JAMES BOSWELL, *Life of Johnson.*

### 177.* THE HAPPINESS OF CHILDREN.

Fresh air and liberty are all that is necessary to the happiness of children. In that blissful age " when nature's self is new," the bloom of interest and beauty is found alike in every object of perception—in the grass of the meadow, the moss on the rock, and the seaweed on the sand. They find gems and treasures in shells and pebbles; and the gardens of fairyland in the simplest flowers. They have no melancholy associations with autumn or with evening. The falling leaves are their playthings; and the setting sun only tells them that they must go to rest as he does, and that he will light them to their sports in the morning. It is this bloom of novelty, and the pure, unclouded, unvitiated feelings with which it is contemplated, that throw such an unearthly radiance on the scenes of our infancy, however humble in themselves, and give a charm to their recollections which not even Tempe can compensate.                T. L. PEACOCK, *Melincourt.*

### 178.** HALLOWED INSTITUTIONS.

Having settled this point to his satisfaction, the doctor stepped down to the hospital, to learn how matters were going on there; and as he walked across the hallowed close, and looked up at the ravens who cawed with a peculiar reverence as he wended his way, he thought with increased acerbity of those whose impiety would venture to disturb the goodly grace of cathedral institutions.

And who has not felt the same? We believe that Mr Horsman himself would relent, and the spirit of Sir Benjamin Hall give way, were those great reformers to allow themselves to stroll by moonlight round the towers of some of our ancient churches. Who would not feel charity for a prebendary, when walking the quiet length of that long aisle at Winchester, looking at those decent houses, and feeling, as one must, the solemn, orderly comfort of the spot? Who can be hard upon a dean while wandering round the sweet close of Hereford, and owning that in that precinct, tone and colour, design and form, solemn tower and storied window, are all in unison, and all perfect? Who could lie basking in the cloisters of Salisbury, and gaze on Jewel's library, and that unequalled spire, without feeling that bishops should sometimes be rich?

ANTHONY TROLLOPE, *The Warden*.

### 179.*** THE CLOISTERED LIFE.

For suddenly there had come to Mary a vision of peace: like a green island in the sea it was, like a white cloud on a broiling day; the sheltered life where all mundane preoccupations were far away, where ambition and hope and struggle were incredibly distant foolishness. Lowly and peaceful and unjaded was that life: she could see the nuns pacing quietly in their enclosed gardens, fingering their beads as they went to and fro and praying noiselessly for the sins of the world, or walking with a solemn happiness to the Chapel to praise God in their own small companies, or going with hidden feet through the great City to nurse the sick and comfort those who had no other comforter than God.—To pray in a quiet place, and not to be afraid any more, or doubtful or despised...!

These things she saw and her heart leaped to them, and of these things she spoke to her mother, who listened with a tender smile and stroked her hair and hands.

But her mother did not approve of these things. She spoke

of nuns with reverence and affection. Many a gentle, sweet woman had she known of that sisterhood, many a one before whom she could have abased herself with tears and love, but such a life of shelter and restraint could never have been hers, nor did she believe it could be Mary's.

For her a woman's business was life ; the turmoil and strife of it was good to be in ; it was a cleansing and a bracing. God did not need any assistance, but man did, bitterly he wanted it, and the giving of such assistance was the proper business of a woman.

JAMES STEPHENS, The Charwoman's Daughter.

### 180.* PATRIOTISM.

Patriotism has always proved the best cordial of humanity, and all the sterner and more robust virtues were matured to the highest degree by its power. No other influence diffuses abroad so much of that steady fortitude which is equally removed from languor and timidity on the one hand, and from feverish and morbid excitement upon the other....It is probable that in the best days of the old classic republics the passions of men were as habitually under control, national tastes as simple and chastened, and acts of heroism as frequent and as grand, as in the noblest periods of subsequent history. Never did men pass through life with a more majestic dignity, or meet death with a more unfaltering calm. The full sublimity of the old classic type has never been reproduced in its perfection, but the spirit that formed it has often breathed over the feverish struggles of modern life, and has infused into society a heroism and a fortitude that has proved the invariable precursors of regeneration.

W. E. H. LECKY, Rationalism in Europe.

### 181.* THE MOTHER-COUNTRY AND THE COLONIES.

My hold of the colonies is in the close affection which grows from common names, from kindred blood, from similar privileges, and equal protection. These are ties, which, though light as air, are as strong as links of iron. Let the colonies always keep the idea of their civil rights associated with your government;—they will cling and grapple to you; and no force under heaven will be of power to tear them from their allegiance. But let it be once understood that your government may be one thing, and their privileges another; that these two things may exist without any mutual relation; the cement is gone; the cohesion is loosened; and everything hastens to decay and dissolution.

As long as you have the wisdom to keep the sovereign authority of this country as the sanctuary of liberty, the sacred temple consecrated to our common faith, wherever the chosen race and sons of England worship freedom, they will turn their faces towards you. The more they multiply, the more friends you will have; the more ardently they love liberty, the more perfect will be their obedience. Slavery they can have anywhere. It is a weed that grows in every soil. They may have it from Spain, they may have it from Prussia. But, until you become lost to all feeling of your true interest and your natural dignity, freedom they can have from none ·but you.        EDMUND BURKE, *Speech on Conciliation.*

### 182.* LIBERTY.

Ariosto tells a pretty story of a fairy, who, by some mysterious law of her nature, was condemned to appear at certain seasons in the form of a foul and poisonous snake. Those who injured her during the period of her disguise were for ever excluded from participation in the blessings which she bestowed. But to those who, in spite of her loathsome aspect, pitied and protected her she afterwards revealed herself in the beautiful and celestial form which was natural to her, accompanied their steps, granted all their wishes, filled their houses with wealth, made them happy in love and victorious in war. Such a spirit is Liberty. At times she takes the form of a hateful reptile. She grovels, she hisses, she stings. But woe to those who in disgust shall venture to crush her! And happy are those who, having dared to receive her in her degraded and frightful shape, shall at length be rewarded by her in the time of her beauty and her glory.

Lord MACAULAY, *Essays.*

## 183.* VALOUR.

It is doubtless very savage that kind of valour of the old Northmen. Snorro tells us they thought it a shame and misery not to die in battle; and if natural death seemed to be coming on, they would cut wounds in their flesh, that Odin might receive them as warriors slain. Old kings, about to die, had their body laid into a ship; the ship sent forth, with sails set and slow fire burning it; that, once out at sea, it might blaze up in flame, and in such manner bury worthily the old hero, at once in the sky and in the ocean! Wild bloody valour; yet valour of its kind; better, I say, than none. In the old Sea-kings too, what an indomitable rugged energy! Silent, with closed lips, as I fancy them, unconscious that they were specially brave; defying the wild ocean with its monsters, and all men and things:—progenitors of our own Blakes and Nelsons!

THOMAS CARLYLE, *Heroes and Hero-Worship.*

## 184.* THE GLORY OF THE HEAVENS.

Believe me, the providence of God has established such an order in the world, that of all which belongs to us, the least valuable parts can alone fall under the will of others. Whatever is best is safest, lies most out of the reach of human power, can neither be given nor taken away. Such is this great and beautiful work of nature—the world. Such is the mind of man, which contemplates and admires the world, where it makes the noblest part. These are inseparably ours; and as long as we remain in one, we shall enjoy the other.

Let us march, therefore, intrepidly, wherever we are led by the course of human accidents. Wherever they lead us, on what coast soever we are thrown by them, we shall not find ourselves absolutely strangers. We shall feel the same revolutions of seasons; and the same sun and moon will guide the course of our year. The same azure vault, bespangled with stars, will be everywhere spread over our heads. There is no part of the world from whence we may not admire those planets, which roll, like ours, in different orbits round the same central sun; from whence we may not discover an object still more stupendous, that army of fixed stars hung up in the immense space of the universe, innumerable suns, whose beams enlighten and cherish the unknown worlds which roll around them ; and whilst I am ravished by such contemplations as these, while my soul is thus raised up to heaven, it imports me little what ground I tread upon.

Lord BOLINGBROKE, *Reflections upon Exile.*

### 185.** LOOKING AT THE SKY.

If, in our moments of utter idleness and insipidity, we turn to the sky as a last resource, which of its phenomena do we speak of? One says, it has been wet ; and another, it has been windy ; and another, it has been warm. Who, among the whole chattering crowd, can tell me of the forms and the precipices of the chain of tall white mountains that girded the horizon at noon yesterday? Who saw the narrow sunbeam that came out of the south, and smote upon their summits until they melted and mouldered away in a dust of blue rain? Who saw the dance of the dead clouds when the sunlight left them last night and the west wind blew them before it like withered leaves? All has passed, unregretted as unseen ; or if the apathy be ever shaken off, even for an instant, it is only by what is gross, or what is extraordinary ; and yet it is not in the broad and fierce manifestations of the elemental energies, nor in the clash of the hail, nor the drift of the whirlwind, that the highest characters of the sublime are developed. God is not in the earthquake, nor in the fire, but in the still small voice.

JOHN RUSKIN, *Modern Painters.*

### 186.** ARCHITECTURE AND NATURE.

Architects ought not to live in our cities; there is that in their miserable walls which bricks up to death men's imaginations, as surely as ever perished forsworn nun. An architect should live as little in cities as a painter. Send him to our hills, and let him study there what nature understands by a buttress, and what by a dome. There was something in the old power of architecture, which it had from the recluse more than from the citizen.  The buildings of which I have spoken with chief praise, rose, indeed, out of the war of the piazza, and above the fury of the populace; and Heaven forbid that for such cause we should ever have to lay a larger stone, or rivet a firmer bar, in our England!  But we have other sources of power, in the imagery of our iron coasts and azure hills, of power more pure, nor less serene, than that of the hermit spirit which once lighted with white lines of cloisters the glades of the Alpine pine, and raised into ordered spires the wild rocks of the Norman sea; which gave to the temple gate the depth and darkness of Elijah's Horeb cave; and lifted out of the populous city, grey cliffs of lonely stone, into the midst of sailing birds and silent air.

JOHN RUSKIN, *The Seven Lamps of Architecture.*

### 187.**** ADORATION.

It is to far happier, far higher, exaltation that we owe those fair fronts of variegated mosaic, charged with wild fancies and dark hosts of imagery, thicker and quainter than ever filled the depth of midsummer dream; those vaulted gates, trellised with close leaves; those window labyrinths of twisted tracery and starry light; those misty masses of multitudinous pinnacle and diademed tower; the only witnesses, perhaps, that remain to us of the faith and fear of nations.  All else for which the builders sacrificed has passed away—all their living interests, and aims, and achievements.  We know not for what they laboured, and we see no evidence of their reward.  Victory, wealth, authority, happiness—all have departed, though bought by many a bitter sacrifice.  But of them and their life and their toil upon the earth, one reward, one evidence, is left to us in those grey heaps of deep-wrought stone.  They have taken with them to the grave their powers, their honours, and their errors; but they have left us their adoration.

JOHN RUSKIN, *The Seven Lamps of Architecture.*

### 188.** TRUE ELEGANCE.

I like a room which looks its best when the sun streams into it through wide open windows and doors   If the furnishing of it cannot stand this test—if it looks uncomfortable under the operation—you may be sure there is something unwholesome about it. As to the question of elegance or adornment, that may safely be left to itself. The studied effort to make interiors elegant has only ended—in what we see.

After all, if things are *in their place* they will always look well. What, by common consent, is more graceful than a ship— the sails, the spars, the rigging, the lines of the hull? Yet go on board and you will scarcely find one thing placed there for the purpose of adornment. An imperious necessity rules every- thing; this rope *could* have no other place than it has, nor could be less thick or thicker than it is, and it is, in fact, this neces- sity which makes the ship beautiful. Everything in it *has rela- tion*—has relation to the winds and waves, or to something else on board, and is there for purposes beyond its own existence.

EDWARD CARPENTER, *England's Ideal.*

### 189.* THE STUDENT'S FIRESIDE.

See how friendly together are the fire and the shaded lamp; both have their part alike in the illumining and warming of the room. As the fire purrs and softly crackles, so does my lamp at intervals utter a little gurgling sound when the oil flows to the wick, and custom has made this a pleasure to me. An- other sound, blending with both, is the gentle ticking of the clock. I could not endure one of those bustling little clocks which tick like a fever pulse, and are only fit for a stock- broker's office; mine hums very slowly, as though it savoured the minutes no less than I do; and when it strikes, the little voice is silver-sweet, telling me without sadness that another hour of life is reckoned.

GEORGE GISSING, *The Private Papers of Henry Ryecroft.*

### 190.* THE LESSON OF EXPERIENCE.

Men are apt enough of themselves to fall into the most astonishing delusions about the opportunities which time affords, but they are even more deluded by the talk of the people about them. When children hear that a new carriage has been

ordered of the builder, they expect to see it driven up to the
door in a fortnight, with the paint quite dry on the panels.

All people are children in this respect, except the workman, who knows the endless details of production; and the
workman himself, notwithstanding the lessons of experience,
makes light of the future task. What gigantic plans we scheme,
and how little we advance in the labour of a day! Three pages
of the book (to be half erased to-morrow), a bit of drapery in
the picture that will probably have to be done over again, the
imperceptible removal of an ounce of marble-dust from the
statue that seems as if it never would be finished; so much
from dawn to twilight has been the accomplishment of the
golden hours. If there is one lesson which experience teaches,
surely it is this, to make plans that are strictly limited, and to
arrange our work in a practicable way within the limits that
we must accept.       P. G. HAMERTON, *The Intellectual Life.*


191.*** LABOUR.

For there is a perennial nobleness, and even sacredness, in
Work. Were he never so benighted, forgetful of his high calling,
there is always hope in a man that actually and earnestly works:
in Idleness alone is there perpetual despair. Work, never so
Mammonish, mean, *is* in communication with Nature; the real
desire to get Work done will itself lead one more and more
to truth, to Nature's appointments and regulations, which are
truth.

The latest Gospel in this World is Know thy work and do
it. "Know thyself": long enough has that poor "self" of thine
tormented thee: thou wilt never get to "know" it, I believe!
Think it not thy business, this of knowing thyself; thou art an
unknowable individual: know what thou canst work at; and
work at it, like a Hercules! That will be thy better plan.

It has been written, "an endless significance lies in Work";
a man perfects himself by working. Foul jungles are cleared
away, fair seedfields rise instead, and stately cities; and withal
the man himself first ceases to be a jungle and foul, unwholesome

desert thereby. Consider how, even in the meanest sorts of Labour, the whole soul of a man is composed into a kind of real harmony, the instant he sets himself to work!

THOMAS CARLYLE, *Past and Present*.


## 192.* OUR STANDARD OF JUDGMENT.

We all have to assume a standard of judgment in our own minds, either of things or persons. A man who is willing to take another's opinion has to exercise his judgment in the choice of whom to follow, which is often as nice a matter as to judge of things for oneself. On the whole, I had rather judge men's minds by comparing their thoughts with my own, than judge of thoughts by knowing who utter them. I must do one or the other. It does not follow, of course, that I may not recognise another man's thoughts as broader and deeper than my own; but that does not necessarily change my opinion, otherwise this would be at the mercy of every superior mind that held a different one. How many of our most cherished beliefs are like those drinking-glasses of the ancient pattern, that serve us well so long as we keep them in our hand, but spill all if we attempt to set them down!

OLIVER WENDELL HOLMES,
*The Autocrat of the Breakfast-Table*.


## 193.** METHOD.

Without care and method the largest fortune will not, and with them almost the smallest will, supply all necessary expenses. As far as you can possibly, pay ready money for everything you buy, and avoid bills. Pay that money, too, yourself, and not through the hands of any servant, who always either stipulates poundage, or requires a present for his good word, as they call it. Where you must have bills (as for meat and drink, clothes, etc.), pay them regularly every month, and with your own hand.

Never, from a mistaken economy, buy a thing you do not

want, because it is cheap; or from a silly pride, because it is dear. Keep an account in a book, of all that you receive, and of all that you pay; for no man, who knows what he receives and what he pays, ever runs out.

I do not mean that you should keep an account of the shillings and half-crowns which you may spend in chair-hire, operas, etc. They are unworthy of the time, and of the ink that they would consume; leave such *minutiae* to dull, penny-wise fellows; but remember in economy, as well as in every other part of life, to have the proper attention to proper objects, and the proper contempt for little ones. A strong mind sees things in their true proportion.

The Earl of CHESTERFIELD, *Letter*, Jan. 10, 1749.

## 194.* THE POWER OF MONEY.

You tell me that money cannot buy the things most precious. Your commonplace proves that you have never known the lack of it. When I think of all the sorrow and the barrenness that has been wrought in my life by want of a few more pounds per annum than I was able to earn, I stand aghast at money's significance. What kindly joys have I lost, those simple forms of happiness to which every heart has claim, because of poverty! Meetings with those I loved made impossible year after year; sadness, misunderstanding, nay, cruel alienation, arising from inability to do the things I wished, and which I might have done had a little money helped me; endless instances of homely pleasure and contentment curtailed or forbidden by narrow means. I have lost friends merely through the constraints of my position; friends I might have made have remained strangers to me; solitude of the bitter kind, the solitude which is enforced at times when mind or heart longs for companion-ship, often cursed my life solely because I was poor. I think it would scarce be an exaggeration to say that there is no moral good which has not to be paid for in coin of the realm.

GEORGE GISSING, *The Private Papers of Henry Ryecroft.*

### 195.*** THAT ALL IS FOR THE BEST.

The frost which kills the harvest of a year, saves the harvests of a century, by destroying the weevil or the locust. Wars, fires, plagues, break up immovable routine, clear the ground of rotten races and dens of distemper, and open a fair field to new men. There is a tendency in things to right themselves, and the war or revolution or bankruptcy that shatters a rotten system, allows things to take a new and natural order. The sharpest evils are bent into that periodicity which makes the errors of planets, and the fevers and distempers of men, self-limiting. Nature is upheld by antagonism. Passions, resistance, danger, are educators. We acquire the strength we have overcome. Without war, no soldier; without enemies, no hero. The sun were insipid, if the universe were not opaque. And the glory of character is in affronting the horrors of depravity, to draw thence new nobilities of power: as Art lives and thrills in new use and combining of contrasts, and mining into the dark evermore for blacker pits of night. What would painter do, or what would poet or saint, but for crucifixions and hells? And evermore in the world is this marvellous balance of beauty and disgust, magnificence and rats.

R. W. EMERSON, *The Conduct of Life.*

### 196.* DELIVERANCE.

Very probably the reader will imagine that we sat up anxiously all night, but the plain truth is that we went to bed soon, and slept as well as possible till the next morning. The excitement of the day had produced that weariness, so common in war-time, which enables people to sleep in perfect tranquillity, notwithstanding the noise of cannon.

The next morning we got up early. The firing had ceased. Men who had been with the Germans all night (for the enemy had occupied their houses) came to tell us that they were in full retreat.

The next time they advanced upon us, the armistice stopped them a few miles from our house. Then the peace came, and we were delivered.

Imagine some tremendous conflagration in the primæval forest, covering thousands of square leagues; it rages and spreads till at length it reaches its limit, and just outside the limit there is a little bird's-nest, with the young in it, and the conflagration ceases, and the nest is not even singed. That nest was like our house. Imagine some fearful inundation, which devastates a hundred towns and more than a thousand farms. It rises and spreads till it goes far inland, and comes near to a little flower. It uproots great trees, and makes many a field like a desert, but that little plant is an inch outside of its course, and the waters subside, and it is just as it was before. Our garden was like that plant.

P. G. HAMERTON, *Round my House* (1876).


## 197.* LASTING PEACE.

Victor and vanquished alike have bravely played their parts. We are above the meanness of jeering over our triumph. They need feel no humiliation in their defeat, and therefore, when the wounds which have been made are healed over, when the scars which have been left begin to fade, then let us see to it as Englishmen worthy of the name that we do nothing to recall the regretted animosities of the past. We must show our readiness to welcome our new fellow-subjects to all the privileges of a greater and a freer Empire than the world has ever known. We must give to them equality in all things with ourselves, and we must ask of them something in return. It is with them now that the future lies. We hold out our hand to them; we ask them to take it, and to take it without any *arrière pensée*, but frankly and in the spirit in which it is offered. Let us try whether out of these two great and kindred races we cannot make a fusion—a nation stronger in its unity than either of its parts would be alone. That is the future of South Africa to which all patriots must aspire, and which is within the bounds of a reasonable aspiration.

JOSEPH CHAMBERLAIN, *Speech at Durban*, Dec. 27, 1902.

### 198.** France and Scotland.

Theologic ink, and Jacobite blood, with gall enough in both cases, seemed to have blotted out the intellect of the country: however, it was only obscured, not obliterated. Lord Kames made nearly the first attempt at writing English; and ere long, Hume, Robertson, Smith, and a whole host of followers, attracted hither the eyes of all Europe.

And yet in this brilliant resuscitation of our fervid genius, there was nothing truly Scottish, nothing indigenous; except, perhaps, the natural impetuosity of intellect, which we sometimes claim, and are sometimes upbraided with, as a characteristic of our nation.

It is curious to remark that Scotland, so full of writers, had no Scottish culture, nor indeed any English; our culture was almost exclusively French. It was by studying Racine and Voltaire, Batteux and Boileau, that Kames had trained himself to be a critic and philosopher; it was the light of Montesquieu and Mably that guided Robertson in his political speculations; Quesnay's lamp that kindled the lamp of Adam Smith. Hume was too rich a man to borrow, and perhaps he re-acted on the French more than he was acted on by them: but neither had he aught to do with Scotland; Edinburgh, equally with La Flèche, was but the lodging and laboratory, in which he not so much morally lived, as metaphysically investigated.        Thomas Carlyle, *Essays.*

### 199.* France.

When wayfaring in France as a tourist the towers of a château seen among the woods from the roadside, or a prefecture standing in its park in a country town, or the modest home of a rural priest beneath the shadow of a church, had always filled me with wondering desire to know what manner of people dwelt within those walls; so having read and imagined much about the lives they led, it would not have been surprising if some disillusion had followed my first entry into this novel society. Nothing of the sort occurred, and the memory of my opening journey as a resident in France is a series of pleasing pictures....

Even now, when I know the French provinces as few foreigners can know them, the familiar scenes of daily life which meet the casual view give me pleasurable sensations as keen as when I was a passing stranger. A bishop blessing little children in the aisles of his cathedral, a group of white-coifed peasant women in a market-place, or a red-legged regiment swinging through a village to the strains of a bugle-march, has now for me not merely the sentimental or picturesque interest of former days. I know, indeed, that the lives of many of these people are neither ideal nor idyllic, but I recognize now in these provincials, with all their failings, the true force of France, which keeps her in the front rank of nations, in spite of the follies, governmental and otherwise, committed in her beautiful capital.          J. E. C. BODLEY, *France*.

### 200.** THE LESSON OF THE CRIMEAN WAR.

Whether the providential purpose of this war be accomplished, must depend on its enabling France and England to love one another, and teaching these, the two noblest foes that ever stood breast to breast among the nations, first to decipher the law of international charities; first to discern that races, like individuals, can only reach their true strength, dignity or joy, in seeking each the welfare, and exulting each in the glory, of the other.

...If France and England fail of this, if again petty jealousies or selfish interest prevail to unknit their hands from the armoured grasp, then, indeed, their faithful children will have fallen in vain; there will be a sound as of renewed lamentation along those Euxine waves, and a shaking among the bones that bleach by the mounds of Sebastopol. But if they fail not of this, if they join in perpetual compact of their different strengths, to contend for justice, mercy, and truth throughout the world, who dares say that one soldier has died in vain? The scarlet of the blood that has sealed this covenant will be poured along the clouds of a new aurora, glorious in that

Eastern heaven; for every sob of wreck-fed breaker round those Pontic precipices, the floods will clap their hands between the guarded mounts of the Prince-Angel; and the spirits of those lost multitudes, crowned with the olive and rose among the laurel, shall haunt, satisfied, the willowy brooks and peaceful vales of England, and glide, triumphant, by the poplar groves and sunned coteaux of Seine.

JOHN RUSKIN, *Modern Painters.*

# INDEX OF AUTHORS

N.B. *The numbers refer to the passages, not to the pages.*

# INDEX OF FIRST WORDS

N.B. *The numbers refer to the passages, not to the pages.*

For EU product safety concerns, contact us at Calle de José Abascal, 56–1°,
28003 Madrid, Spain or eugpsr@cambridge.org.

www.ingramcontent.com/pod-product-compliance
Ingram Content Group UK Ltd.
Pitfield, Milton Keynes, MK11 3LW, UK
UKHW012339130625
459647UK00009B/390